BY FELIX A. LORENZ

"The only hope for the Laodiceans is a clear view of their standing before God, a knowledge of the nature of their disease."

Ellen G. White,
Testimonies for the Church, Vol. 4, p. 87.

THE ONLY HOPE

Southern Publishing Association, Nashville, Tennessee

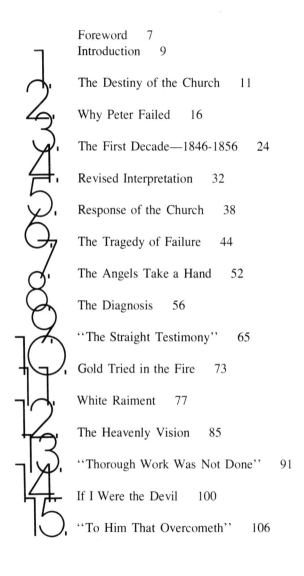

Foreword

This book, THE ONLY HOPE, by Felix A. Lorenz, will never be forgotten by those who read it. It is the product of a lifetime of Bible study and research in the Spirit of Prophecy. It is the urgent cry of an earnest and consecrated heart. It comes to us as fellow believers with a tremendous challenge. It contains an excellent condensation of the story of the 1888 message of righteousness by faith and the appeal of the True Witness to the church of Laodicea in the latter days. It is, in brief, the spiritual history of the remnant church concentrated in fifteen short chapters. It describes days of encouragement, of standstill, of advance, of retreat, of failures and darkness. But the last chapter describes the final and certain and glorious victory of the people of God.

The author has given us a documented and chronological record of the Lord's appeal for doctrinal and spiritual revival and reformation from the year 1848 to the present. The Biblical foundations are very strong, and I would like to call especial attention to the statement of the prophecy on the seven churches of Revelation 2 and 3, with emphasis on the Laodicean message as applied to the experience of the remnant church.

The author has had wide experience in Bible teaching in a number of educational institutions, and his special ability in this field is clearly evident. His use of the appropriate Spirit of Prophecy material is unique—in that the various messages on his chosen topic are arranged in chronological order, together with a brief historical picture of the church from one critical period to another up to our present situation.

This book brings to us the most relentless and convicting, yet the most hopeful and stirring appeal for the reception and proclamation of the Lord's message to Laodicea that I have ever read or heard. It is full of Scripture, full of the Spirit of Prophecy, and full of love. May it be used of God to the blessing of the church in these days and of all our hearts as well.

H. M. S. RICHARDS

Introduction

While director of Lay Activities in the Kansas Conference of Seventh-day Adventists, I became deeply concerned about my own spiritual status and that of my church after studying what Ellen G. White had to say about the Laodicean message. As time went on, I discussed my concern with many of my fellow ministers, some of them in the General Conference, and many of them urged me to write a book on the subject.

Then when I had to choose a theme for a dissertation for my Bachelor of Divinity degree at the Theological Seminary in 1951, I asked permission to write on the subject. The dean, Dr. Charles E. Weniger, approved my request. LeRoy E. Froom served as faculty adviser, and I wrote under the title ''A Study of the Laodicean Message With Emphasis on the Writings of Mrs. E. G. White.''

Since that time it has been my privilege to teach the subject matter of the dissertation in two of our colleges. Many of the more mature students insisted that I must write a book on the subject. And now, retired and with more time at my disposal, I undertook the task.

Soon after the emphasis on Laodicea first came to the church in 1856, Mrs. White warned that ''the destiny of the church hangs'' on preaching it, and that at that time it had ''been lightly esteemed if not entirely disregarded.'' To what extent could that be true today? This book will examine that question.

9

1. The Destiny of the Church

The city lay hushed in sleep. A full Passover moon hung overhead, revealing the tented slopes crowded with multitudes of pilgrim worshipers. One could hear nothing except the occasional bleating of a sacrificial lamb. To the east, on the crest of the Mount of Olives, Jesus stood, beholding the familiar scene. For fifteen long centuries the Jews had made their annual pilgrimage here, looking forward to the appearance of the Coming One, who would fulfill all their Messianic hopes. And here He watched, the living substance which the Passover only symbolized. They had waited so long for Him. And now He had arrived.

But they did not know it.

Just three years later, He would pass the same mountain, approach the same city, riding in triumph—but weeping —saying, "If thou hadst known, even thou, at least in this thy day, the things which belong unto thy peace!" (Luke 19:42).

But they did not know.

He had tried to bring the knowledge of salvation to His chosen people through the prophets, finally saying through Isaiah, "The ox knoweth his owner, and the ass his master's crib: but Israel doth not know" (Isaiah 1:3). Scripture portrays the cause of Israel's final rejection thus: "My people are destroyed for lack of knowledge" (Hosea 4:6). But they could have known.

Suddenly Christ sensed that He was not alone. Perhaps He heard a twig snap. Peering into the darkness, He saw someone

11

approaching. As the stranger drew nearer, Jesus recognized him as a Pharisee—a rich Pharisee, judging by his expensive garments. He was a ruler of the Jews, a representative of the religious establishment.

Nicodemus—the night visitor—had observed the obscure Galilean and the events of the past few days. Impressed, he now wanted to show his sincere interest. "Rabbi, we know——" As a representative of the chosen people, he should have said, "We know that You are the promised Messiah, and what Israel needs is salvation!" But Nicodemus didn't. He didn't know that. And it disappointed Jesus. Nicodemus acknowledged Him as come from God, but a teacher, not the Messiah.

Sweeping aside the visitor's flattering approach, his high social status, his official standing of leadership in the church —disregarding it all—Jesus went right to the crucial point. What we need to talk about is you, Christ told him, not Me— you as an individual, and you as a representative of the church. You need to be born again, born anew, born from above. And you will find rebirth by looking at Me, just as your forefathers obtained healing by gazing at the bronze serpent. That is what Isaiah meant when he said, "Look unto me, and be ye saved, all the ends of the earth" (Isaiah 45:22). Yes, Nicodemus, your one need, Israel's need, the need of all mankind, is conversion—full and true conversion—and that comes only from Me.

Nicodemus was humiliated. "He felt that he needed no change. Hence his surprise at the Saviour's words. He was irritated by their close application to himself" (*The Desire of Ages,* p. 171). When he mused, "How can these things be?" Jesus replied in surprise, "Art thou a master [teacher] of Israel, and knowest not these things?" (John 3:9, 10).

With His mild rebuke Jesus laid His finger on the problem of Nicodemus and of the Hebrews as a whole. They were solely responsible for their final failure. That they were sinners and needed a Saviour they partially realized. But that the Messiah was to save His people from their sins only a few faintly sensed. Such a transformation must come about by personal salvation from sin—by conversion.

None of them seemed to grasp that fact at all.

Jesus told Nicodemus, "Except a man be born again, he cannot see the kingdom of God." The Greek passage does not use *blepō*, "to see with the eyes," but *horaō*, which also means, "to see with the mind, perceive, discern" (Abbott Smith, *Manual Greek Lexicon of the New Testament*, p. 321.

After quoting the words of Jesus to Nicodemus, Mrs. White paraphrases them: "You must have the divine mold before you can discern the sacred claims of the truth" (*Selected Messages, Book One*, p. 412). Jesus is not speaking of seeing with the eyes the glories of the kingdom, but of discerning with spiritual vision "the sacred claims of the truth." Again Mrs. White says, "He cannot discern the requirements essential to having a part in that spiritual kingdom." She called it "the very alphabet of conversion" (*Fundamentals of Christian Education*, p. 459). Jesus stated it in the plural, "Ye must be born again," thus directing it to the entire church.

Christ honored Nicodemus' desire for secrecy. He never betrayed his confidence. Many years later, after Nicodemus had learned the truth of conversion, he perhaps related the experience to John, who recorded it in his Gospel. The same John the Beloved, after another thirty years had passed, became a prisoner on the Isle of Patmos during one of the persecutions, probably that of Domitian.

One Sabbath day he had a vision. Christ instructed him to write it out and send it to the seven churches in Asia. Tradition suggests that John served as the undershepherd of the Christian church in that part of southwestern Asia Minor then known as Asia. Naturally he would be especially interested in the churches of his personal parish. But it could seem strange that he should address only seven of them when we know more existed. The well-known church of the Colossians was also in Asia but not included.

The number seven dominates the symbolism of the entire Book of Revelation—the churches, the seals, the trumpets, the thunders, the plagues. Scholars have long regarded the seven churches as symbols of stages or conditions of the Christian church. L. E. Froom lists "in rapid summarizing, . . . some two thousand years of cumulative application" of prophetic interpretations, and among them he mentions "the seven churches, seals, and trumpets, covering the Christian Era" (*The Prophetic Faith of our Fathers,* Vol. IV, pp. 205, 206). Ellen G. White comments, "The names of the seven churches are symbolic of the church in different periods of the Christian Era" (*The Acts of the Apostles,* p. 585). It has been the official position of the Seventh-day Adventist Church since the autumn of 1856.

Adventists traditionally apply the church of Ephesus to the Apostolic period, from its founding until the death of the last apostles about AD 100. Then follows Smyrna, the church of the persecution, which we see as ending with the time of Constantine. Next is Pergamos, representative of the period of greatest apostasy, extending from about 323 to 538, when the Papacy became a secular political power. After that, during the time of the church of Thyatira, we find the acknowledged people of God generally outside the established church, a situation we may designate as the church in the wilderness. With the Protestant Reformation the condition of the church of Sardis appears and continues from about 1517 to 1800, when the worldwide "Advent awakening" introduces the church of the revival, the church of Philadelphia. The last stage of the church is Laodicea, which will continue until the return of Christ.

John received a special, personal message for each church. In most cases the messages contained both approval and censure. Two—Smyrna and Philadelphia—had no rebuke directed toward them. And only one among the seven had no commendation. And that is the Laodicean church—God's people today.

The rebukes are stern and unequivocal. But Christ spoke them in love and tenderness, and they offer courage and hope. The saddest, most tragic, note in the letter to Laodicea is that it does not know its true condition. It says, "I am rich, and increased with goods, and have need of nothing."

Jesus, who introduces Himself here as the True Witness, states, "You don't know, but I do. You really think that you need nothing at all. But in reality you are 'wretched, and miserable.' Why? Because you are 'poor, and blind, and naked.' Now I have remedies for all three maladies. However, they are not available to you as long as you think you are 'rich, and increased with goods, and have need of nothing.' "

Ellen G. White declares that the Laodiceans have "only one hope"—the preaching of the Laodicean message. On it hangs "the destiny of the church."

2. Why Peter Failed

The conference president's voice trembled with emotion as he bared his heart to the approximately one hundred ministers, Bible instructors, and office employees in his conference. A retired minister had come to visit his young preacher son who was serving in his first pastorate. The annual workers' meeting had convened, and the conference president had kindly invited the visiting minister to attend it.

On the last morning the president gave the devotional study. He registered deep concern as he discussed with his staff the problems of the ensuing year. "We can never finish the spread of the gospel in this large state with our handful of ministers and Bible instructors," he told them. "There must be a great program of lay evangelism that will harness the full potential of all our church members. The task of inspiring and promoting that movement falls upon us sitting here today.

"During this year we shall have to raise hundreds of thousands of dollars to support our own conference, our local and union conference institutions, and our worldwide missions. That, too, will be the responsibility of every one of us here.

"Then there is another matter that I would rather not have to mention at all. You may go into any church in this conference, and if you stay long enough and dig deeply enough, you will find rivalries, jealousies, and friction. The Lord will never come to take us home with Him until we have banished all such hatred by His spirit of selflessness and love.

"All this, my dear fellow workers, we must do this year

besides our regular duties of revival and evangelism.''

The meeting adjourned at noon, and the father and son went home. While the daughter-in-law prepared their noon meal, they retired to the young preacher's study. ''Did you notice your president's four bases of concern in the devotional study this morning?'' the father asked. ''Take down your Volume 9 of the *Testimonies* from the shelf there.

''You remember his first burden was for a revival of evangelism on the part of the entire membership of the church. Now please notice the next to the last sentence on page 30.''

'' 'He who is truly converted will be so filled with the love of God that he will long to impart to others the joy that he himself possesses,' '' his son read.

''What does the church need, Son, to produce such a missionary spirit?''

''It seems it is true conversion,'' the younger man replied.

His father remembered the years he had spent in several conferences as Lay Activities secretary, trying almost vainly to stimulate just such a lay program. ''His second concern was financial,'' he continued. ''Now please look at the first two sentences of the middle paragraph on page 53.''

'' 'Those who are truly converted will regard themselves as God's almoners, and will dispense, for the advancement of the work, the means He has placed in their hands. If Christ's words were obeyed, there would be sufficient means in His treasury for the needs of His cause.'

''Dad,'' the young preacher said, ''wouldn't that be wonderful—always enough funds for all needs? No more pressuring and pleading from the pulpit—if we were truly converted.''

''The third problem your president presented was one that has always plagued the church. The same remedy is its only solution. Read it on page 147, still in Volume 9, the seventh line from the top.''

" 'Those who are truly converted will press together in Christian unity.' "

"Your president's last emphasis involved the regular evangelistic activities of the ministry. Here, too, you will find that the same problem calls for the same answer. Turn to Volume 6 and read the sentence beginning on line five on page 371."

" 'The Lord does not now work to bring many souls into the truth, because of the church members who have never been converted, and those who were once converted but who have backslidden.' "

By now the young minister had become persuaded that the need of the church was true or full conversion. And it was necessary not only in his conference, but in the church generally. Hopefully his discovery did not leave him too distressed or discouraged. In fact, a careful study of the experience of Christ's disciples should reassure His people today.

Jesus called His disciples to be His followers and finally His heralds because they were good men. But we will see that being good men is not enough. Even good men must become converted men, transformed by and into the life of their Saviour. Here is the formula for salvation.

They spent three years in intimate communion with Him— thirty-six months. That is four times nine months—a full college course—with the greatest teacher the world has ever known. If they did not graduate with honors, it certainly wasn't their Instructor's fault.

During their senior year, a little more than six months before graduation time, He introduced to them a new and important subject—new to the disciples, but not to Jesus. Nearly three years before, He had tried to tell Nicodemus all about it.

They neared the end of His six-month ministry in and around Galilee, usually spoken of as "the special training of the twelve." Six months later He would die on the cross. In response to Jesus' searching question, "Whom do men say that I am?" Peter had made his memorable response, "Thou art the Christ." It was then that Jesus initiated a fuller revelation of Himself and His mission. "And he *began* to teach them, that the Son of man must suffer many things, and be rejected of the elders, and of the chief priests, and scribes, and be killed, and after three days rise again" (Mark 8:31).

With conclusive finality He stated that His enemies would kill Him, and after three days He would rise from the dead. Weren't they listening? At least Peter heard Him say it, for he began to rebuke Him, "This shall not be unto thee" (Matthew 16:22). Jesus recognized Peter's unwillingness to follow in His steps of sacrifice. He perceived the source of his spirit and identified it. "Get thee behind me, Satan," He commanded, and then proceeded to reveal to the disciples and the rest of the multitude the unequivocal terms of discipleship. "If any man will come after me, let him deny himself, and take up his cross, and follow me" (verse 24). Surely if they had listened at all, they could hardly forget so startling a statement.

But they did. Even Peter forgot after one short week. As they came down from the Mount of Transfiguration, Jesus enjoined Peter and the sons of Zebedee not to mention the night's events "till the Son of man . . . [was] risen from the dead." They looked at each other in blank amazement, "questioning one with another what the rising from the dead should mean" (Mark 9:9, 10). Christ's words made no sense to them.

Another week or two passed, and Jesus and His disciples returned from the area of Caesarea Philippi, north of Galilee, to their home at Capernaum. Again Jesus broached the subject. "He taught his disciples, and said unto them, The Son of man is delivered into the hands of men, and they shall kill him; and after that he is killed, he shall rise the third day." Simple, forthright words, nothing obscure or mysterious about them. "But they understood not that saying" (Mark 9:31, 32).

We will permit Luke to tell it as he received it. And note the three consecutive verses as he records them. "Let these sayings sink down into your ears: for the Son of man shall be delivered into the hands of men. But they understood not this saying." Why couldn't they understand? Does the next verse explain it? "There arose a reasoning among them, which of them should be greatest" (Luke 9:44-46). Is there a causal relation found in these three verses? Did their lust for leadership obscure spiritual truth? One of the basest passions of human nature is the desire to rule others.

At least three months went by before the next recorded mention of Jesus' approaching death. He and His disciples were in Perea, east of the Jordan. Once again He attempted to penetrate their blind minds, now more explicitly and in greater detail.

"Then he took unto him the twelve, and said unto them, Behold, we go up to Jerusalem, and all things that are written by the prophets concerning the Son of man shall be accomplished. For he shall be delivered unto the Gentiles, and shall be mocked, and spitefully entreated, and spitted on: and they shall scourge him, and put him to death: and the third day he shall rise again" (Luke 18:31-33). Surely now the twelve men, ordained to the ministry by Jesus Himself, soon to be entrusted with the sacred task of telling the world of salvation—surely now they would begin to fathom the meaning of it all. But the next verse says simply, "And they understood none of these things: and this saying was hid from them, neither knew they the things which were spoken."

Jesus and His disciples returned to Jerusalem. It was the last week before His crucifixion. He continued to warn them by explicit allusions to His approaching death. "Ye know that after two days is the feast of the passover, and the Son of man is betrayed to be crucified" (Matthew 26:2). Then when Mary broke the alabaster box of ointment, He said, "For in that she hath poured this ointment on my body, she did it for my burial" (verse 12). At the first Communion service, He told His disciples, "This is my body," and "This is my blood" (verses 26, 28). Finally, just before they left the upper room, Jesus announced, "But after I am risen again, I will go before you into Galilee" (verse 32). "Truly the Son of man goeth, as it was determined: but woe unto that man by whom he is betrayed!" (Luke 22:22). How could such statements fail to register with them? The answer appears in verse 24: "And there was also a strife among them, which of them should be accounted the greatest."

After the Crucifixion, eleven brokenhearted men found their way back to the upper room where just the night before they had received the symbols of a death and resurrection they did not yet understand. Surely one of them should have remembered and reminded the other ten that they should expect a risen Master in three days. But no one did. And after Mary Magdalene burst into the room and announced to the eleven that He was indeed alive and had sent a message to them, "when they had heard that he was alive, and had been seen of her, believed not" (Mark 16:11).

Jesus delayed His return to heaven another forty days to give the disciples another opportunity. He concentrated on the subject in which they had failed most completely, "speaking of the things pertaining to the kingdom of God" (Acts 1:3). Nearly two years before, Jesus had tried to teach them "the mysteries of the kingdom of heaven" (Matthew 13:11), but they did not grasp it. Would they understand now?

The day came when a cloud would carry Him out of their sight. But He had two things to declare before He could leave them. The first revealed their total failure *without* Him. The second proclaimed their complete final triumph *with* Him.

It would seem that after forty additional days on the one

theme of the kingdom, they would now have fully understood it all. But just before He departed, "they asked of him, saying, Lord, wilt thou at this time restore again the kingdom to Israel?" (Acts 1:6). It is difficult to imagine the disappointment that their flagrant ignorance must have inflicted on Him. And yet He knew that all their ignorance and blindness would be fully provided for.

And that brings in Christ's second declaration during the last moments before the ascension. Notwithstanding the disciples' complete failure to comprehend the mysteries of His kingdom, despite His often-repeated teachings, He assured them that, under the guidance of the Holy Spirit, He would lead them into all truth.

"But ye shall receive the power of the Holy Ghost coming upon you [margin]: and ye shall be witnesses unto me" (Acts 1:8). "I shall not be here to correct your theology. But I am willing to stake the success of the great plan to rescue fallen man, which I have provided with My own life—I am willing to stake it all on the work of poor, fallible man, plus the direction of the Holy Spirit. I know that man can do nothing alone. You men have demonstrated that, and don't ever forget it. But I also know that you same frail and faulty men, when controlled by the Holy Spirit, will be adequate for all tasks and problems."

Three full years had not enabled the disciples, even under the Master's teaching, to understand the most elemental concepts. But ten days of repentance and confession and full conversion, under the power of the Holy Spirit, made them fit revelations to the world of the divine Lord and His truth. The experience explained to them what Jesus had meant when He said that it would be much better for them that He should go away so that the Spirit of truth could come to them.

When the day of Pentecost fully arrived, the Holy Spirit passed by the guileless Nathaniel, the beloved John and his brother James, and laid His hand on the shoulder of Simon

Peter, the greatest sinner of the lot, to preach the great dedication sermon of the gospel movement and the Christian church. And He did it to show to men and women of all times what God can do with a man who, in true repentance, permits God to empty him of self and fill him with the life and love of Jesus.

Peter had thought that he was ready for his assignment in the Lord's service. He wasn't. Instead he was all wrapped up with the interests of Simon Peter. Every effort and opportunity went to further himself. But Jesus told him that after his conversion he should strengthen, not himself, but his fellow believers. And he did just that. After his full conversion he became a new man. Not a vestige of the old self-seeking, proud Simon remained. Conversion will do the same for the church today.

Just what is conversion? Jesus described it to Nicodemus as a spiritual rebirth. Paul called it a dying to the natural or fallen self, a becoming a new creature (Romans 6:2-8; 2 Corinthians 5:17). It is the inexplicable result of the Spirit. Man's sole part is the decision, the surrender of his stubborn, selfish will. God does all the rest. Perhaps one of the most important facts about conversion is that it is cumulative, a daily experience. The disciples of Jesus became truly or fully converted in the upper room before Pentecost. Then the power came. That will also be the experience of the Laodiceans. It will bring another Pentecost, power in witnessing, and personal victory (*Testimonies to Ministers,* p. 50).

"We must see our need of a physician. We are sick, and do not know it. May the Lord convert the hearts of His workmen! When there is a converted ministry, then look for results" (*Pacific Union Recorder,* August 14, 1902).

"When the character of Christ shall be perfectly reproduced in His people, then He will come to claim them as His own" (*Christ's Object Lessons,* p. 69).

3. The First Decade – 1846·1856

The Adventists fully expected that the Lord would return to earth on October 22, 1844. They were disappointed. But we must not ascribe it solely to a deficient spiritual condition, for the evidence of a rich and deep experience among many at that time is abundant.

Mrs. Ellen G. White was not only an eyewitness and a participant, she also had divine insight that would render her appraisal of spiritual things accurate. A group of statements from her writings will reveal the spiritual tone of many of the believers just before October, 1844.

"We carefully examined every thought and emotion of our hearts, as if upon our deathbeds and in a few hours to close our eyes forever upon earthly scenes" (*Testimonies,* Vol. 1, p. 51).

"With diligent searching of heart and humble confessions we came prayerfully up to the time of expectation. Every morning we felt that it was our first work to secure the evidence that our lives were right before God. Our interest for one another increased; we prayed much with and for one another" (*ibid.,* p. 55).

"We frequently went to the orchards and groves, and sent up our earnest cries to God, 'Restore unto us the joys of thy salvation.' We would not cease pleading with the Lord until he revealed himself unto us, and we could rejoice in the sweet assurance of his love" (*Spiritual Gifts,* Vol. 2, p. 29).

Speaking of her own experience during those days of anxious waiting, Mrs. White says, "This was the happiest year of

my life'' (*Testimonies,* Vol. 1, p. 54). She indicates that the
''little flock'' came through October, 1844, with courage and
peace in their hearts. Discussing it, she says, ''We were disappointed, but not disheartened'' (*ibid.,* p. 56).

The year 1848 was the year of the six Sabbath conferences.
While the Sabbath had taken root in a small way before, now
it became the great issue, and to spread it the infant church began
publishing tracts and pamphlets. In July, 1849, appeared the
first issue of *Present Truth.* Ten more followed. Then, from
August until November of 1850 came the five numbers of *The
Advent Review.* A survey of the articles they carried will reveal
that they emphasized the Sabbath. But it seems that the attention
on the Sabbath crowded out proper attention to nurturing the
believers in spiritual growth. Also, the certainty of being right
generates complacence and spiritual pride.

Four years later saw the expansion of their publishing.
James White launched *The Youth's Instructor,* and Adventists
acquired their first printing press. Always the battle for the true
Sabbath continued. In 1853 the Whites made their first journey
to Michigan and carried on despite poverty and sickness
(*Testimonies,* Vol. 1, pp. 91-93). Then came the year 1854 and
the troubles with the Messenger Party (*ibid.,* pp. 95, 96). The
church's leaders moved printing facilities to Battle Creek in
1855 (*ibid.,* p. 97). And so the ten years since the Sabbath
doctrine had come to the leaders passed, and what had it done
for the developing church?

At the conference held in Battle Creek, May 27, 1856, Mrs.
White witnessed in vision ''some things that concern the church
generally'' (*ibid.,* p. 127). In her view of ''The Two
Ways''—the title she gave the vision—she saw that ''those who
travel in the narrow way are talking of the joy and happiness
they will have at the end of the journey. Their countenances are
often sad, yet often beam with holy, sacred joy.'' But she also
observed that many were actually journeying ''in the broad

way, yet they professed to be of the number who were traveling the narrow way" (*ibid.*, pp. 127, 128). She contrasted the spirit before October, 1844, and that of the present. "Then I was pointed back to the years 1843 and 1844. There was a spirit of consecration then that there is not now," she exclaimed. "What has come over the professed peculiar people of God?" (*ibid.*, p. 128).

It was not the first time that God revealed to her the little church's spiritual deterioration, nor the first occasion that she had warned it.

The first section of *Early Writings*—"Experience and Views"—went to press in 1851. Within its seventy or more pages we find such reproofs, but they emphasize the lack of spiritual growth and progress rather than retrogression:

"Dear Brethren: The Lord gave me a view, January 26, 1850, which I will relate. I saw that some of the people of God are stupid and dormant and but half awake" (page 48).

"The mighty shaking has commenced and will go on, and all will be shaken out who are not willing to take a bold and unyielding stand for the truth and to sacrifice for God and His cause" (page 50).

"At Oswego, New York, September 7, 1850, the Lord showed me that a great work must be done for His people before they could stand in the battle in the day of the Lord" (page 69).

"May 14, 1851, . . . I also saw that many do not realize what they must be in order to live in the sight of the Lord without a high priest in the sanctuary through the time of trouble. Those who receive the seal of the living God and are protected in the time of trouble must reflect the image of Jesus fully" (pages 70, 71).

In the June 10, 1852, issue of *The Review and Herald,* Mrs. White wrote, "As I have of late looked around to find the humble followers of the meek and lowly Jesus, my mind has been much exercised.

"Many who profess to be looking for the speedy coming of Christ, are becoming conformed to this world, and seek more earnestly the applause of those around them, than the approbation of God. They are cold and formal, like the nominal church, that they but a short time since separated from. The words addressed to the Laodicean Church, describe their present condition perfectly."

The second section of *Early Writings,* called the "Supplement," appeared in 1854. In it she stated, "I saw that the remnant were not prepared for what is coming upon the earth. Stupidity, like lethargy, seemed to hang upon the minds of most of those who profess to believe that we are having the last message" (page 119).

Following a long paragraph condemning the habit of magnifying trials, nursing grievances, and justifying self, she adds, "Pride has crept in among Sabbathkeepers—pride of dress and appearance. Said the angel, 'Sabbathkeepers will have to die to self, die to pride and love of approbation' " (page 120).

The year 1855 saw the beginnings of what is now the nine-volume set of *Testimonies for the Church,* by Mrs. E. G. White. On the fifth of May she had a vision which she introduced by saying, "I saw that there was a great lack of faith with the servants of God, as well as with the church. They were too easily discouraged, too ready to doubt God, too willing to believe that they had a hard lot and that God had forsaken them" (*Testimonies,* Vol. 1, p. 120).

But the message that struck with explosive force at the complacence and security of the church came in a vision which Mrs. White had in November, 1855, on the last day of a three-day conference held at the "House of Prayer" at Battle Creek. A report of it became the first part of *Testimony Number One,* Volume 1. At its close, below Mrs. White's signature, appeared the following notes:

"We, the undersigned, being eye-witnesses when the above

vision was given, deem it highly necessary that it should be published, for the benefit of the Church, on account of the important truths and warnings which it contains.

"Jos. Bates,	M. E. Cornell,
"J. H. Waggoner,	J. Hart,
"G. W. Amadon,	Uriah Smith.

"NOTE.—The above vision was read before thirty-six members of the Battle Creek Church, on the evening of Nov. 24th, who gave their unanimous vote for its publication. It can be had by addressing E. G. White, Battle Creek, Mich. Those who would encourage the circulation of such matter, can do so by assisting in its publication. S. T. BELDEN" (*Testimony for the Church, Number One,* 1855 edition, p. 8).

The *Review and Herald's* report of it appeared in the December 4 issue:

"Held at the 'House of Prayer' at Battle Creek, Nov. 16th-19th, was a meeting of importance and deep interest. Brn. Hart of Vt., Bates of Mass., Belden of Conn., and Waggoner, lately from Wis., and a goodly number from different parts of this state, were present. Nov. 16th was spent in transacting business expressed in the call for the Conference. Sabbath, 17th, in a most thorough examination and discussion of the time to commence the Sabbath; 18th, three discourses were given by Brn. Waggoner and Bates; 19th, in prayer, and remarks, and confessions relative to the evident departure of the remnant from the spirit of the message, and the humble, straightforward course taken by those who first embraced it. Strong desires were expressed, and fervent prayers were offered to heaven, for the return of the spirit of consecration, sacrifice and holiness once enjoyed by the remnant. Our longsuffering and tender Father in heaven smiled upon his waiting children, and manifested his power to their joy. The brethren separated greatly refreshed and encouraged" (Editorial, "The Conference," *Review and*

Herald, December 4, 1855, p. 75).

It is quite the usual procedure to discuss the items of business on the first day of the meeting, as happened here. But it is unusual that the delegates would spend the Sabbath on a theoretical or theological question, ''in a most thorough examination and discussion of the time to commence the Sabbath,'' while Monday, the last day, finds them in the grip of a spiritual revival. One would expect it to come on the Sabbath.

The complete change of tone on the final day of the meeting may have been the conference's response to the message that Heaven had sent them through Mrs. White's vision. Because of prejudice, the *Review and Herald* did not discuss her vision directly at that time, and the statement that the ''Father in heaven smiled upon his waiting children, and manifested his power to their joy'' may have been a veiled allusion to the vision.*

''I saw that the Spirit of the Lord has been dying away from the church,'' Mrs. White told them. ''The servants of the Lord have trusted too much to the strength of argument, and have not had that firm reliance upon God which they should have. I saw that the mere argument of the truth will not move souls to take a stand with the remnant; for the truth is unpopular.

''The servants of God must have the truth in the soul. Said the angel: 'They must get it warm from glory, carry it in their bosoms, and pour it out in the warmth and earnestness of the soul to those that hear.' A few that are conscientious are ready to decide from the weight of evidence; but it is impossible to move many with a mere theory of the truth. There must be a power to attend the truth, a living testimony to move them.

Note: November 20 in 1855, the date given for the vision, was Tuesday. But the last day of the conference was Monday. If indeed James White's statement that the ''Father in heaven smiled upon his waiting children, and manifested his power to their joy'' referred to it, then the vision took place on November 19 instead of 20.

"I saw that the enemy is busy to destroy souls. Exaltation has come into the ranks; there must be more humility. There is too much of an independence of spirit indulged in among the messengers. This must be laid aside, and there must be a drawing together of the servants of God. There has been too much of a spirit to ask, 'Am I my brother's keeper?' Said the angel: 'Yea, *thou art* thy brother's keeper. Thou shouldest have a watchful care for thy brother, be interested for his welfare, and cherish a kind, loving spirit toward him. Press together, press together' " (*Testimonies,* Vol. 1, pp. 113, 114).

Her statement deserves some analysis and detailed study. She made the following charges:

1. The influence of the Spirit of the Lord had been dying out of the church.

2. Too many had relied on argument.

3. Such preaching brings in only a few conscientious ones.

4. To preach with power, "they must get it warm from glory."

5. Too much independence had come "among the messengers," the ministers.

6. They must lay it aside.

7. "Said the angel: 'Yea, *thou art* thy brother's keeper.' "

It seems she directed the rebuke largely at the ministers. The offense seems to be the tendency to ask, "Am I my brother's keeper?" It must be that such an attitude of unconcern among the ministry is a significant and revealing symptom of spiritual retrogression.

But she does not spare the rest of the church, for she goes on to say, "I saw that the church has nearly lost the spirit of self-denial and sacrifice; they make self and self-interest first, and then they do for the cause what they think they can as well as not. Such a sacrifice, I saw, is lame, and not accepted of God" (*ibid.,* p. 115). Her message was brief—three pages—but it seems all the more poignant for its shortness. The last part of

Testimony Number One, "Prepare to Meet the Lord," appeals to young people, reminding them that the angel with scales is weighing their thoughts (*ibid.,* pp. 124, 125).

The following spring another conference convened at Battle Creek. Again Mrs. White received a vision in which she witnessed "some things that concern the church generally" (*ibid.,* p. 127). Her account of it bears the title, "The Two Ways." After describing the two classes of people on earth, she adds, "What has come over the professed peculiar people of God? I saw the conformity to the world, the unwillingness to suffer for the truth's sake. I saw a great lack of submission to the will of God" (*ibid.,* p. 128).

Testimony for the Church, Number Two, which contained the preceding passage, came out during the summer of 1856. The first notice of its publication appeared in the *Review and Herald* of August 21, page 128. The second of the three articles comprising it has the title "Conformity to the World." We will quote only one passage: "As I saw the dreadful fact that God's people were conformed to the world, with no distinction, except in name, between many of the professed disciples of the meek and lowly Jesus and unbelievers, my soul felt deep anguish. I saw that Jesus was wounded and put to an open shame" (*Testimonies,* Vol. 1, p. 133).

Twelve years had passed since October, 1844. And it is a tragic picture indeed to see the men and women who believed and endured so faithfully before and after the 1844 disappointment, now grown into a much larger and well-organized church, but proud, selfish, and complaining, while still claiming to be the Philadelphia church, the church of brotherly love, and still condemning the poor Laodiceans, the non-Sabbath-observing Adventists.

4. Revised Interpretation

By early October, 1856, the infant church had become a healthy, growing organism. It had achieved unity on doctrinal investigation and formation. All visible prospects seemed bright and promising. What more could the young church desire?

Then came the disillusionment. Mrs. White solemnly proclaimed rebukes and warnings—often spoken in the exact words of the ''accompanying angel''—that the church had lost its former hold on God. According to the angel, ''the Spirit of the Lord has been dying away from the church,'' and in bewildered sorrow she asked, ''What has come over the professed peculiar people of God?''

Through its leaders, the church had committed itself to the theory that it was in the Philadelphian state, the church of brotherly love, and those who had opposed her were the Laodiceans. Now how would they reconcile their traditional position with Mrs. White's reproof? Obviously the Philadelphian condition did not fit the church. It was equally plain that it would be painful and humiliating to retreat from the old and accepted view.

What could James White, the editor of the church organ, the *Review and Herald,* do? How would the membership respond to a radical change in interpretation on the last two of the seven churches? We can only imagine his intense meditation on the subject, his fervent prayers, his long and troubled consultations with his wife. But he made his decision.

When the *Review and Herald* came from the press bearing the date of October 9, 1856, it contained on page 184 a brief editorial composed mostly of questions and signed by James White:

"Watchman, What of the Night?"

"The inquiry is beginning to come up afresh, 'Watchman, what of the night?' At present there is space for only a few questions, asked to call attention to the subject to which they relate. A full answer, we trust, will soon be given.

"1. Do the seven churches (Rev. 1:11) represent seven conditions of the true church, in seven periods of time?

"2. If so, then is the view erroneous that the Philadelphia and Laodicean states both exist at the same time?

"3. Does 'the church in Sardis' represent the nominal churches to whom the Advent Message was first given?

"4. And does 'the church in Philadelphia,' represent the church of God in her state of consecration and 'brotherly love,' looking for the coming of Jesus in 1844?

"5. If so, is not the present time the period for the Laodicean condition of the church?

"6. Does not the state of the Laodiceans (lukewarm, and neither cold nor hot) fitly illustrate the condition of the body of those who profess the Third Angel's Message?

"7. Are not the nominal churches, and the nominal Adventists (as bodies) to all intents and purposes, 'cold'?

"8. Then where is the 'lukewarm' church, unless it be those who profess the Third Message?

"9. And is not this our real condition as a people?

"10. Does not the prophecy answer perfectly to the facts?

"11. If this be our condition as a people, have we any real grounds to hope for the favor of God unless we heed the 'counsel' of the 'True Witness,' as follows?'' Then he quoted Revelation 3:18-21.

The obvious implication of his questions must have stunned the church. Whether James White had discussed the subject with other church leaders before he published his list of questions, we do not know. In the next issue of the *Review and Herald* he wrote about the subject again.

"Laodicea signifies," he said, " 'the judging of the people,' or, according to Cruden, 'a just people,' and fitly represents the present state of the church, in the great day of atonement, or judgment of the 'house of God' while the just and holy law of God is taken as a rule of life.

"It has been supposed that the Philadelphia church reached to the end. This we must regard as a mistake, as the seven churches in Asia represent seven distinct periods of the true church, and the Philadelphia is the sixth, and not the last state. The true church cannot be in two conditions at the same time, hence we are shut up to the faith that the Laodicean church represents the church of God at the present time.

"The conditional promises to the Philadelphia church are yet to be fulfilled to that portion of that church who comply with the conditions, pass down through the Laodicean state, and overcome.

"But, dear brethren, how humbling to us as a people is the sad description of this church. And is not this dreadful description a most perfect picture of our present condition? It is; and it will be of no use to try to evade the force of this searching testimony to the Laodicean church. The Lord help us to receive it, and profit by it. What language could better describe our condition as a people, than this addressed to the Laodiceans? 'Neither hot nor cold,' but 'lukewarm.' It will not do, brethren, to apply this to the nominal churches, they are to all intents and purposes, 'cold.' And the nominal Adventists are even lower than the churches, who justly look down upon them with horror for the infidel views, held by many of them, of no Sabbath, no family worship, no Devil, no operation of the Holy

Ghost, no pre-existence of the Son of God, and no resurrection of the unjust'' (''The Seven Churches,'' *Review and Herald,* October 16, 1856, p. 189).

The *Review and Herald* of November 6 included two letters, one from a leading minister, the other from a layman. Stephen N. Haskell wrote from Princeton, Massachusetts, that he had been thinking along lines identical with White's for some time, so the new position did not come to him as a surprise (''A Few Thoughts on the Philadelphia and Laodicean Churches,'' *ibid.,* November 6, 1856, p. 6).

The layman was a Battle Creek man named David Hewitt. When Joseph Bates first came to Battle Creek, the postmaster directed him to Hewitt as ''the most honest man in town.'' After expressing himself in harmony with the view that applies the Laodicean message to the Adventist Church, he ended with the plea, ''Dear brethren and sisters, can we not see from the nature of the petition that the lovely Jesus is not in our hearts, though we have supposed he was? O let him in. Fathers and mothers, let him in. Husbands and wives, let him in. Young men and women, let him in. Children, let him in. Preachers, let him in. May the writer of this let him in'' (''Gold Tried in the Fire,'' *ibid.,* p. 2).

The following week James White had a full-page article in the *Review* entitled ''The Laodicean Church.'' It was a detailed exposition of the last part of Revelation 3, showing how it fitted the condition of the developing Adventist Church (November 13, 1856, p. 13). In the November 20 issue, page 20, White addressed a letter to the church. It carried the heading ''An Appeal to Those Who Profess the Third Angel's Message,'' and begins, ''Dear Brethren:—We are fully convinced that the rebuking testimony to the Laodiceans is addressed to those who profess to keep the Commandments of God and the Faith of Jesus.'' He then outlined in detail what he felt the church should do to merit having the ''faith of Jesus'' but made no further reference to the Laodicean message.

And so James White at first challenged the accepted position on the seven churches, applied the message to his own church, then made a careful exposition of the first three chapters of Revelation. Finally he outlined in detail in his open letter to the members what he felt the church should do to correct the situation. A careful reading of it reveals that White believed that "love for this present world, and the acquirement of riches, is the great sin that is drowning the present generation in perdition," and adds that it "is doubtless one of the greatest causes of grieving the Spirit of God away from the remnant" (*ibid.*).

By the end of November, the new position had become the official stand of the church. But, as far as the records show, Mrs. White had not said one word on the subject. The first notice of the publication of *Testimony for the Church, Number Three,* appeared in the *Review and Herald* of April 30, 1857, six months after James White first challenged the old interpretation of the seven churches.* It proved to be the shortest Testimony in the nine volumes—thirteen pages—and contained only two articles. The first carried the title "Be Zealous and Repent," coming from the center of the Laodicean passage of Revelation. The first paragraph begins, "Dear Brethren and Sisters: The Lord has shown me in vision some things concerning the church in its present lukewarm state, which I will relate to you. The church was presented before me in vision. Said the angel to the church: 'Jesus speaks to thee, "Be zealous and repent" ' " (*Testimonies,* Vol. 1, p. 141).

Mrs. White couched the entire section in the phraseology of the Laodicean message. And the passage indicates that Mrs. White agreed with her husband that "love of the world" and

---

* *Note:* The publication date, as shown on page 713, is 1856, whereas the *Comprehensive Index to the Writings of Ellen G. White,* Volume III, page 3194, gives the publishing date as 1857. It seems reasonable to believe that she wrote Testimony Three near the beginning of 1857.

"earthly treasures" were to a large degree responsible for the spiritual condition of the church, but she also condemns fault-finding. Another passage states, "Heed the counsel of the True Witness. Buy gold tried in the fire, that thou mayest be rich, white raiment that thou mayest be clothed, and eyesalve that thou mayest see. Make some effort. These precious treasures will not drop upon us without some exertion on our part. We must buy—'be zealous and repent' of our lukewarm state. We must be awake to see our wrongs, to search for our sins, and to zealously repent of them" (*ibid.*, p. 142).

Through such plain-spoken statements Mrs. White joined her husband and others in applying the Laodicean message to the church's membership.

5. Response of the Church

The reversal of the church in its position on the application of the Laodicean message had been sudden and radical. The little body, snug in its newfound faith and ardent in defending it, had felt secure in God's favor under the symbolism of the Philadelphian church. And then suddenly they saw their assurance swept away, and the church faced the withering and unequivocal rebuke of God. His message had not a word of approbation to soften the blow. Would they rise in defiance, or would they bow in humble submission?

On the ninth of October the challenge went out. And by the twentieth of November the new view had become an established doctrine. The *Review and Herald* was the church organ and encouraged letters from its readers. They responded freely to the question of Laodicea. The letters to the *Review* constituted the most accurate criterion of how readily the church accepted the changed position.

During the fourteen months from November, 1856, through the year 1857, 348 items appeared in the *Review* on the Laodicean message. Of them, James White or other editorial writers accounted for sixteen. Seventy came from ministers, the other 262 from lay members. In view of the small number of Sabbath observers at the time, it represented a large response.

It is most revealing to examine them. The 348 contributions contain not a single dissent, and the ministers indicated general acceptance among the churches. A careful study of all the statements would be interesting and highly revealing. But space permits only a few typical items.

The ministers had recognized the waning spirituality of the churches. In November J. H. Waggoner wrote, "I feel constrained to add my testimony as to the lukewarm condition of the professed Sabbath-keepers. This fact has long been a deep grief to me. Especially have I been burdened with the state of those who have for years professed the faith" (*Review and Herald*, November 20, 1856, p. 24).

A month later Frederick Wheeler said something similar: "That a lukewarm state has come over the church, is a fact too plainly seen to be denied. The worldly spirit that is seen, the lack of consecration, and of the spirit and power that marked the early progress of the Third Angel's Message, are too apparent, and tell that it is even so" ("Ye Are the Light of the World," *ibid.*, December 18, 1856, p. 54).

But the ministers could report real progress among the churches under the preaching of the Laodicean message. R. F. Cottrell reported in December, "These scattered brethren have set apart the second Sabbath in each month for meeting together in one place to break bread. We had a refreshing season. The testimony to the Laodicean church was considered, and all seemed willing to receive the rebuke of the True Witness, and be zealous and repent" (*ibid.*, December 25, 1856, p. 61). "I have scarcely heard a dissenting voice to the testimony which shows the Laodicean Sabbath keepers to be in a lukewarm state," S. W. Rhodes said (*ibid.*, January 8, 1857, p. 78). And A. S. Hutchins added, "I wish here to add that a happy change is taking place among us. The solemn and stirring message to us, Laodiceans, is arousing the Church to action *now*" ("Conference at Wolcott, Vt.," *ibid.*, p. 80).

Equally positive are the reports that came from the laymen. David Arnold from Fulton, New York, sent quite a long letter to the December 18, 1856, *Review* (page 55). His interpretation of the three symbolic remedies recommended by the True Witness is noteworthy though premature when compared with the definitions that Mrs. White later attached to them.

The following week a letter arrived from H. H. Wilcox. It stressed a common human weakness—applying God's rebukes to others. "I should like to say through the *Review* that I am thankful that faithful brethren through whom the Lord could work have apprised us of our lukewarm state. I saw that this was our condition, when it was first advocated through the *Review;* but notwithstanding I saw that we were mistaken in giving this to the nominal Adventists, yet I was too willing to give it to my brethren and sisters, as though others were more needy than myself; but in this I was sadly mistaken. I am thankful that whilst I was in this deplorable condition, Brn. Rhodes and Goodwin came, and through their labors I was led to see that I was the man addressed and counseled to buy gold" (*ibid.,* December 25, 1856, p. 63).

Wilcox saw even at first the message's true meaning and application, yet it did him no good because he relegated it to others—a common and dangerous practice. It took the minister through the spoken word to make him conscious of his own need. The same attitude stands out in the letter from Mary L. Priest—that she did not feel the appeal's influence until she received it from the minister (*ibid.,* February 19, 1857, p. 127).

J. Dorcas wrote to the editor, "Bro. Smith: Permit me to say that Bro. Cornell has been down here among us in Ohio, 'in the demonstration of the Spirit and with power,' so that we cheerfully acknowledge that his work has been the work of God. We have not only been faithfully advised of our true condition as the Laodiceans; but I wish here to humbly confess that I have been made to feel my truly abhorrent character before God. I have seen clearly that pride and selfishness have been mixed with all that I have done" (*ibid.,* February 26, 1857, p. 135).

It is significant that when he began to feel his abhorrent character before God, pride and selfishness stood out prominently in his mind. His reaction harmonizes with Mrs. White's statement in *Steps to Christ* that "pride, selfishness, and covetousness too often go unrebuked. But these are sins that are especially offensive to God" (page 30).

A suggestion of what might have happened, had the Laodicean message accomplished its goal, appears in a letter from E. R. Seaman, who stated, "He [Christ] says he will come in and sup with us. I have proved and know him true. The spirit of our meeting at Boston has shown the same to every one present. The same spirit that we had in 1843-4, was with us, and the last work is commenced that will end in glory if we are faithful. But it will cost all we have and are" (*Review and Herald*, March 19, 1857, p. 159).

It seems that not everybody accepted the new interpretation on the Laodicean church with the same vigor or at the same time. The new Adventist colony at Waukon, Iowa, particularly hesitated. In the *Review* of January 15, 1857, James White, reporting his visit to Waukon, commented about the members there: "They were generally rejecting the testimony to the Laodiceans, which would be calculated to separate them in feeling and interest from the body of the brethren. In this state of things we could not expect to be received by all these friends as affectionately as formerly, yet we were received and cared for with Christian courtesy" ("Western Tour," p. 84).

A vision at Round Grove, Illinois, prompted Mrs. White to make the two-hundred-mile trip to Waukon by sleigh through snow and storm. Arriving there, Mrs. White abruptly greeted J. N. Loughborough, "What doest thou here, Elijah?" Fifty years later Loughborough recorded the incident. After describing the coming of the Whites, he discussed the Laodicean question. "Those giving the 'Laodicean message' were teaching that the seven churches of Revelation referred to the seven stages of the Gospel Church from the days of the apostles down to Christ's second coming, and that the seventh state—the

Laodicean—was in the time of the 'judgment of the people.' . . .

"The second day of the meetings Sr. White was in vision for more than half an hour. O, the solemn presence of God that pervaded our midst, melting all hearts to tenderness and contrition. . . . As one after another would take their stand for the truth of this timely Laodicean message, the power of God would come upon them" (Loughborough, "Sketches of the Past, No. 102," *Pacific Union Recorder,* August 18, 1910, pp. 5, 6).

Two of the most impressive of the many responses came from leading ministers. M. E. Cornell observed, "Since I received the message to the Laodiceans, I have been led to consider with deep humiliation, the wrongs of my past life. . . . My example has not been right, I have been forward in precept, but my 'good works,' have not shone out. I have been destitute of the gold. I am ashamed of my past mismovements, and feel to heartily repent before God. I ask the forgiveness and prayers of all I have in any way grieved. I mean to make clean work, and arise with the remnant" ("Confession," *Review and Herald,* February 5, 1857, p. 109).

"I think in some degree, since the stirring counsel to the Laodiceans began to be preached, I have been awakened to a sense of my situation," A. S. Hutchins said. "I have confessed, and still do humbly confess, my great lack of patience, my want of meekness, and of Christian forbearance toward the erring, in the past; also my severity of language in administering reproofs and admonitions. The Lord abundantly pity, and freely forgive me, is my prayer; and the dear children of God also" ("Communication From Bro. Hutchins," *ibid.,* April 9, 1857, p. 184).

Such statements from two of the leading ministers must have had a sobering and challenging effect on any Seventh-day Adventist who read them. Certainly, if all the ministers and all the lay members of that time had found the same experience and made the same consecration that they did, the church would have progressed greatly. But unfortunately that was not the case. James White sounded a discouraging note.

"Our solemn and settled convictions are that the testimony to the Laodiceans has not been felt and obeyed as it will be by those who walk in the path of present truth," he observed. "It has been too much of a surface work, the influence of which soon passes from many minds. . . . The Spirit of the Lord came down upon us on Sabbath afternoon, and the Lord there plead [sic] with his people, as it were, face to face. The testimony given was that the counsel to the Laodiceans had not been fully heeded; that the work had not been deep; but in many cases a surface work" ("Eastern Tour," *ibid.,* June 4, 1857, p. 36).

6. The Tragedy of Failure

One cannot determine the success or failure of an enterprise until he establishes an authentic norm of what constitutes success. To ascertain whether the Laodicean message that came to the church in the fall of 1856 accomplished its appointed purpose, we must compare its results with its goal. We can illustrate that by a historical incident.

The Whites started their winter journey to Waukon, Iowa, from Round Grove, Illinois. They had remained with the little Adventist colony at Round Grove "several weeks, holding meetings, recovering and strengthening the brethren there." In addition, they convened a conference of all Illinois Adventists. "Everts and Hart [who accompanied the Whites] took hold with renewed faith and enthusiasm" (Arthur Whitefield Spalding, *Captains of the Host,* p. 257). The new emphasis the Whites held should have transformed the Round Grove church. Yet Elder M. E. Cornell writes in December, 1857, just one year later, "Bro. Smith: The Lord is blessing our efforts here in Illinois. The first Sabbath after leaving Battle Creek, we met with the church in Round Grove, Whiteside Co. . . . Our united effort resulted, we believe, in much good; tears flowed freely, and that sorrow manifested that we trust will produce reform. There had been a great lack of brotherly love—the spirit of 'am I my brother's keeper' still prevailed there, and instead of faithfulness to admonish an erring brother, his faults had been talked over with others, until there was a general lack of confidence, and brotherly love, and fellowship was nearly gone" (*Review and Herald,* December 24, 1857, p. 54).

The experience of the Round Grove church seems typical of the entire body of believers—a wonderful revival of "several weeks" under the ministry of the Whites in December and January, and "a great lack of brotherly love" until "fellowship was nearly gone" just one year later.

As early as June, while on a tour of Adventist congregations in the northeastern United States, James White complained of the way the lukewarm church had neglected their duty toward the Hutchins family, who were serving in Vermont. "Bro. and Sr. Hutchins were at home. Our communion with these dear friends, especially around the family altar, was sweeter than language can describe. As we saw Bro. and Sr. Hutchins, pale, care-worn and much wasted in flesh and strength, our fears were aroused: . . . that a lukewarm, worldly church had suffered them to bear burdens grievous [sic] to be borne" (James White, "Eastern Tour," *ibid.,* June 25, 1857, p. 61).

"June 10th a large room-full of brethren and sisters assembled at Bro. Barrows', to whom we spoke with some freedom on the *present* position of believers in the present truth. A few only seem anxious to follow the light while they have it.

"The 13th and 14th, we joined the brethren in their general Tent-meeting which was held in Morristown. The gathering was large. We spoke twice on the Sabbath on the subject of the Seven Churches and the judgment with some freedom; but with little effect upon the large congregation of professed believers. We were more than ever satisfied that but few Sabbath-keepers have received into their hearts the testimony to the Laodiceans" (*ibid.*).

In September A. S. Hutchins contrasted the attitude in which Adventists had at first received the teaching on Laodicea and the indifference they now manifested toward it. He said, "When the light first shone out on this subject, it was set home most powerfully by the Spirit of God, to the hearts of those who acknowledged and received its proper application. We felt indeed that we were wretched, and miserable, and poor, and blind and naked, and that there *must* be a speedy reform, a deep and hearty consecration to God. Many were zealous in the work of repentance. . . .

"But for a time past I have been led to ask the question, what has become of the counsel to the Laodiceans? Why is there so little said on this subject? And why no more feeling? We ask why? What means the stupor, the calm that has come over the people of God?" ("Counsel to the Laodiceans," *ibid.,* September 3, 1857, p. 141).

One could cite many more examples. Begun with such promising prospects, and at first received with such enthusiasm, the reformation lost its momentum and power in a few short months. Mrs. White confirmed what was happening to the developing church. On November 20, 1857, she had a vision that portrayed clearly God's full plan for the giving of the Laodicean emphasis right through all the subsequent conditions and events, ending with Christ's return. We will now carefully analyze Mrs. White's report of her important vision.

First she saw "the people of God" in two separated groups. One prayed intensely. She describes the scene vividly. "Some, with strong faith and agonizing cries, were pleading with God. Their countenances were pale, and marked with deep anxiety, expressive of their internal struggle. Firmness and great earnestness were expressed in their countenances, while large drops of perspiration fell from their foreheads" (*Testimonies,* Vol. 1, pp. 179, 180).

The other group also belonged to "the people of God." "Some, I saw, did not participate in this work of agonizing and pleading. They seemed indifferent and careless. They were not resisting the darkness around them, and it shut them in like a thick cloud. The angels of God left these, and I saw them hastening to the assistance of those who were struggling with all their energies to resist the evil angels, and trying to help themselves by calling upon God with perseverance. But the angels left those who made no effort to help themselves, and I lost sight of them'' (*ibid.*, pp. 180, 181).

It is a tragic picture. They were God's people. They doubtless prayed, but not ''in this work of agonizing and pleading.'' Their great problem—indifference and carelessness. The result—''I lost sight of them.''

The first group, however, rose to their feet and began moving ''in exact order, firmly, like a company of soldiers'' (*ibid.*, p. 181). ''They had obtained the victory,'' she says, and then she follows them in vision as they ''speak forth the truth in great power''—such power that she asks her accompanying angel what had produced the great change. ''It is the latter rain,'' the angel answered, ''the refreshing from the presence of the Lord, the loud cry of the third angel'' (*ibid.*, pp. 182, 183). The next scene depicted the anger and fury of the wicked because ''the zeal and power with the people of God had aroused and enraged them'' (*ibid.*, p. 183). Then follows a period when ''every one, without an exception, was earnestly pleading and wrestling for deliverance,'' suddenly interrupted by ''the voice of God which shook the heavens and the earth'' and the coming of Christ (*ibid.*, pp. 183, 184).

But what precipitated the rapidly moving chain of events? Those in prayer. And what drove them to their knees? ''I asked the meaning of the shaking I had seen,'' Mrs. White said, ''and was shown that it would be caused by the straight testimony called forth by the counsel of the True Witness to the Laodiceans'' (*ibid.*, p. 181).

Then she pronounced the verdict of Heaven on the church's response. ''The testimony of the True Witness has not been half heeded. The solemn testimony upon which the destiny of the church hangs has been lightly esteemed, if not entirely disregarded'' (*ibid.*).

The solemn scenes of her vision reveal what might have been, what in the plan of God should have been. The fact that such events did not follow the message indicates that it did not succeed according to the divine purpose.

Why did it fail? During 1858, Mrs. White was not well physically and greatly perplexed mentally (*ibid.*, p. 185). In 1859 *Testimony Number Five* appeared, and the first section bore the title, "The Laodicean Church." In it she admitted that the message did not do its work. The entire article contains reasons and explanations as to why it did not succeed more fully. It will be profitable, certainly, to list them. But first, a few quotations on the collapse of the Laodicean message:

"The message to the Laodiceans has not accomplished that zealous repentance among God's people which I expected to see, and my perplexity of mind has been great" (*ibid.*).

"If the counsel of the True Witness had been fully heeded, God would have wrought for His people in greater power" (*ibid.*, p. 186).

Following appear some of the reasons she gave for its failure:

"I was shown that the testimony to the Laodiceans applies to God's people at the present time, and the reason it has not accomplished a greater work is because of the hardness of their hearts" (*ibid.*).

"Nearly all believed that this message would end in the loud cry of the third angel. But as they failed to see the powerful work accomplished in a short time, many lost the effect of the message" (*ibid.*).

"Many moved from feeling, not from principle and faith, and this solemn, fearful message stirred them. It wrought upon their feelings, and excited their fears, but did not accomplish the work which God designed that it should" (*ibid.*, p. 187).

"Some are willing to receive one point; but when God brings them to another testing point, they shrink from it and stand back, because they find that it strikes directly at some cherished idol'' (*ibid.*).

"If any will not be purified through obeying the truth, and overcome their selfishness, their pride, and evil passions, the angels of God have the charge: 'They are joined to their idols, let them alone,' and they pass on to their work, leaving these with their sinful traits unsubdued, to the control of evil angels'' (*ibid.*).

"Professors of religion are not willing to closely examine themselves to see whether they are in the faith; and it is a fearful fact that many are leaning on a false hope'' (*ibid., p.* 188).

"Your pride, your love to follow the fashions of the world, your vain and empty conversation, your selfishness, are all put in the scale, and the weight of evil is fearfully against you'' (*ibid., pp.* 189, 190).

"Many, I saw, were flattering themselves that they were good Christians, who have not a single ray of light from Jesus. They know not what it is to be renewed by the grace of God'' (*ibid., p.* 190).

"The greatest sin which now exists in the church is covetousness. God frowns upon His professed people for their selfishness'' (*ibid., p.* 194).

The message that should have driven the church to its knees in the kind of praying described in the November 20, 1857, vision had failed. Why? Because of "the hardness of their hearts," because "they failed to see the powerful work accomplished in a short time," because of "some cherished idol." They refused to let God purify them from "their selfishness, their pride, and evil passions." Instead they were "leaning on a false hope" that their profession would save them. "Your pride, your love to follow the fashions of the world, your vain and empty conversation, your selfishness," she warned, are "against you."

We must include one more observation that Mrs. White

made on the failure of the message. The *Review* of June 16, 1859, had announced *Testimony Number Five*. In September of the following year Volume 2 of *Spiritual Gifts* appeared (James White, "Spiritual Gifts, Vol. 2," *Review and Herald,* September 18, 1860, p. 144). Chapter 31 has the title "The Laodicean Testimony" and contains an almost verbatim restatement of the chapter in *Testimony Number Five* from which we took the preceding quotations. However, it has a preamble which begins, "In the spring of 1857, I accompanied my husband on a tour East. His principal business was to purchase the Power Press. We held conferences on our way to Boston, and on our return. This was a discouraging tour. The testimony to the Laodicean church was generally received; but some in the East were making bad use of it. Instead of applying it to their own hearts, so as to be benefited by it themselves, they were using the testimony to oppress others" (*Spiritual Gifts,* Vol. 2, pp. 222, 223).

One of the most comprehensive single paragraphs Mrs. White ever wrote on the subject occupies most of page 186 of *Testimonies for the Church,* Volume 1. A thorough examination of it will answer a number of vital questions, including that of the church historians who say they cannot account for the great revival of 1857 and 1858 among American Protestant churches.

The statement discusses the collapse of the Laodicean message which came to the church with such glowing promise and ended so suddenly in little more than a year. We must carefully consider seven facts.

1. First, she assures the church that even at the date of her writing, more than two years after the Laodicean message arrived, "the testimony to the Laodiceans applies to God's people at the present time."

2. "The reason it has not accomplished a greater work is because of the hardness of their hearts."

3. "As they failed to see the powerful work accomplished in a short time, many lost the effect of the message. I saw that this message would not accomplish its work in a few short months."

4. "Nearly all believed that this message would end in the loud cry of the third angel."

5. "But God has given the message time to do its work." It appears that instead of "a few short months," it would have required at least a little more than two years.

6. "This fearful message will do its work." As much as to say, if it is not done in your time and in your hearts, God will still accomplish it during the time and in the lives of some future people of His. But, Mrs. White assures us, "this fearful message will do its work."

7. God had a right to expect His people to fulfill His high and holy purposes in His message, so "angels were sent in every direction to prepare unbelieving hearts for the truth." God dispatched the angels, and they went everywhere.

7. The Angels Take a Hand

The young church's failure is a sad spectacle. But it becomes even more tragic when we discover all that it involved. It concerned not only the church's experience with God, but the fact that God had already begun preparing the general population to respond to an Adventist church that should have fully accepted the Laodicean warning.

The American religious awakening of 1800, which had really begun a decade earlier, "continued for a full half century in an almost unbroken succession of revivals, thereby constituting an era of evangelism unparalleled in the history of the nation or the world" (Frank G. Beardsley, *Religious Progress Through Religious Revivals*, p. 39). Then it stopped. Contemporary observers did not know why.

"From 1843 to 1857," the church historian Beardsley has written, "there were several years during which the accessions to the churches scarcely equalled the losses sustained by death and discipline.

"The Great Revival [of 1857], moreover, was preceded by a period of financial and commercial prosperity unprecedented in the history of our country. . . . Thus it was that the 'cares of this world, and the deceitfulness of riches, and the lusts of other things' so preoccupied the minds of men that they became utterly indifferent to the claims of religion" (*A History of American Revivals*, pp. 215, 216).

Then came the collapse which Warren A. Candler has described: "Riches increased, and multitudes set their hearts upon them. Political strife grew more bitter, and the great Civil War drew on apace. In the midst of all its plenty and pride, the nation woke one morning to find the glory was all a dream. While speculation was at a fever-heat and when men were wild with a mania for money-making, there came a financial crash unprecedented in the nation's history. In the twinkling of an eye the riches of many took wings and flew away. Bankruptcies, failures, frauds and defalcations were on every hand, and the hearts of men failed them for fear.

"And now that the wheels of industry stood still and the noisy cries of greed were hushed, men stopped to hear the voice of the Spirit calling them to repentance. And they heeded the heavenly call. Another revival of national extent began" (*Great Revivals and the Great Republic,* pp. 189, 190).

It was not a church-sponsored revival. "The preaching of the gospel has indeed been the principal means made use of in promoting these mass movements in religion, and yet in the Great Revival of 1857-1858 preaching seems to have occupied a very secondary place," Beardsley reports, "for the saving power of the gospel at that time received its chief emphasis through the personal testimony of the men and women whose hearts God had touched" (*Religious Progress Through Religious Revivals,* p. 176).

Nor did God resort to the power of the pulpit, which had in all other revivals held such a prominent place. "It did not begin in the churches," Candler states, "nor was it brought to pass by the preaching of some long-neglected doctrine of grace, as had been the case in all the national revivals that had preceded it" (page 190).

Church historian Candler here emphasizes that aspect of the revival that most surprised him, and should be to the Laodicean church the most challenging: it was not "brought to pass by the preaching of some long-neglected doctrine of grace."

Candler and Beardsley did not know that "angels were sent

in every direction to prepare unbelieving hearts for the truth." A long-neglected doctrine indeed should have accompanied the revival—the body of teachings implied in Revelation 14. If the Adventists had responded to their opportunity, it would have led to the return of Jesus. But "because of the hardness of their hearts," and because "they failed to see the powerful work accomplished in a short time," they "lost the effect of the message."

God had indeed sent the angels "in every direction," and He could not fail those who had responded. So He found an obscure layman—a businessman—and through him and many more like him He ministered to those under the influence of the revival. The fact that the Laodicean message came to the church late in 1856, and that the revival began without explanation within the next year we cannot dismiss as a coincidence.

It was a lay movement. We need not repeat here the well-known story of the midday prayer meetings in the heart of New York City started by businessman Jeremiah C. Lanphier (Beardsley, *A History of American Revivals*, pp. 218-221). "The good work thus begun in New York quickly spread to Philadelphia, Boston and other cities and towns, until there was scarcely a place of any considerable importance in the United States in which similar services were not undertaken" (Candler, p. 192).

Another writer noted its vast extent. "Then [1857] the Northern States enjoyed another great general revival which visited all parts of the English-speaking world. It was a 'Revival With a Million Converts' " (Arthur B. Strickland, *The Great American Revival*, pp. 132, 133). As one might expect in a laymen's movement, "the methods employed for the further-ance of this work were the distribution of tracts, personal work, and the daily union prayer meetings" (Beardsley, *A History of American Revivals*, p. 231).

The revival spread so rapidly and moved with such power

that "for the time being politics, casualties, crime, and the various secular interests of the day were overshadowed by the news of the revival, telegraphic reports of which were given prominence in the daily press. When the revival was at its height, the New York *Herald* and other papers published extras giving the lastest news of the revival from various parts of the country" (Beardsley, *Religious Progress Through Religious Revivals,* pp. 48, 49).

A religious journal of the day carried the following pen picture during March, 1858: "Such a time as the present was never known since the days of the Apostles, for revivals. The prostration of business, the downfall of Mammon, the great god of worship to the multitudes in this land, both in and out of the church, the sinfulness and vanity of earthly treasures, as the supreme good, have come home to the hearts and consciences of the millions in our land with a power that seems irresistible. Revivals now cover our very land, sweeping all before them, as on the day of Pentecost, exciting the earnest and simultaneous cry from thousands, What shall we do to be saved? . . . The large cities and towns generally from Maine to California are sharing in this great and glorious work. There is hardly a village or town to be found where a special divine power does not appear to be displayed. It really seems as if the Millennium was upon us in its glory" (Henry C. Fish, *Handbook of Revivals,* pp. 77, 78).

But where were the great churches that should have led the way? And where was the Laodicean church?

The most encouraging thought that we can present here is that "this fearful message will do its work." Sometime, some generation of God's church will respond to the appeal of the Laodicean message. God will again send the angels out in every direction to prepare unbelievers. And the people of God, under His power, will prepare the world for the return of their Lord. "This fearful message will do its work." That is a promise.

8. The Diagnosis

Over a decade passed, and Mrs. White received another view of the church which she described in Volume 2 of her *Testimonies for the Church* series. It appeared in a fifty-page discussion under the caption "An Appeal to the Church." She began by saying, "October 2, 1868, I was shown the state of God's professed people. Many of them were in great darkness, yet seemed to be insensible of their true condition" (page 439). Toward the close of the chapter she mournfully declared, "I have waited anxiously, hoping that God would put His spirit upon some and use them as instruments of righteousness to awaken and set in order His church. I have almost despaired as I have seen, year after year, a greater departure from that simplicity which God has shown me should characterize the life of His followers. There has been less and less interest in, and devotion to, the cause of God." And she ended the long appeal by warning that "it will be more tolerable for Sodom and Gomorrah" than for many in the church (pages 484, 488).

More than five years passed, and Volume 3 appeared. In the middle of it, beginning *Testimony Number Twenty-three,* we find another message headed "The Laodicean Church." Written in 1873, it again applied Revelation 3:14-18 to the church. "The message to the church of the Laodiceans is a startling denunciation, and is applicable to the people of God at the present time" (*Testimonies,* Vol. 3, p. 252).

Three years later, in 1876, she reaffirmed, "The Laodicean message applies to the people of God who profess to believe present truth. The greater part are lukewarm professors, having a name but no zeal" (*ibid.*, Vol. 4, p. 87).

In May, 1882, Mrs. White produced "An Appeal" to be read at the camp meetings. The first paragraph and two others follow:

"I am filled with sadness when I think of our condition as a people. . . . Grievous and presumptuous sins have dwelt among us. And yet the general opinion is that the church is flourishing and that peace and spiritual prosperity are in all her borders" (*ibid.*, Vol. 5, p. 217).

"The church has turned back from following Christ her Leader and is steadily retreating toward Egypt. Yet few are alarmed or astonished at their want of spiritual power" (*ibid.*).

"Again and again has the voice from heaven addressed you. Will you obey this voice? Will you heed the counsel of the True Witness to seek the gold tried in the fire, the white raiment, and the eyesalve?" (*ibid.*, p. 233).

Eighteen long years elapsed before the next volume of the *Testimonies*, Volume 6, came from her pen. The years witnessed the unfolding of righteousness by faith at the 1888 Minneapolis meeting. And the long stay of Mrs. White in Australia ended just after Volume 6 appeared. Viewing the church that she had seen, eighteen years before, "steadily retreating toward Egypt," what did she find? As she beheld the meager results of its evangelism, she declared, "The Lord does not now work to bring many souls into the truth, because of the church members who have never been converted and those who were once converted but who have backslidden" (*ibid.*, Vol. 6, p. 371). And then, as she scrutinized the spiritual life of the church, she added, "Today a large part of those who compose our congregations are dead in trespasses and sins. They come and go like the door upon its hinges" (*ibid.*, p. 426). The church had heard solemn warnings now for more than a half century. Why could they not see it? Mrs. White answered, "There is a stupor, a paralysis, upon the people of God which prevents them from understanding what is needed for this time'' (*ibid.,* p. 445).

Two years later, in 1902, Volume 7 came off the press. Devoted largely to church institutions and their growth and to the activities of the departments of the church, it also has its words of warning. Speaking to parents concerning their neglected duty toward their children's spiritual welfare, Mrs. White urged them to ''no longer remain in the condition of the Laodicean church'' (*ibid.,* Vol. 7, p. 67).

Early in the same year, in the *Review and Herald,* she wrote, ''God brings against ministers and people the heavy charge of spiritual feebleness, saying, 'I know thy works, that thou art neither cold nor hot: I would thou wert cold or hot. . . .'

''God calls for a spiritual revival and a spiritual reformation. Unless this takes place, those who are lukewarm will continue to grow more abhorrent to the Lord, until He will refuse to acknowledge them as His children.

''A revival and a reformation must take place, under the ministration of the Holy Spirit'' (Ellen G. White, ''The Need of a Revival and a Reformation,'' *Review and Herald,* February 25, 1902, p. 385).

In her article Mrs. White connected the Laodicean message with a need for revival and reformation—the former, the malady; the latter, the remedy. Mrs. White had now discussed the problem more than fifty years. From then on she seldom made direct mention of the Laodicean warning, but frequently spoke about the solution.

Volume 8, published in 1904, contains one brief chapter of less than five pages, ''Shall We Be Found Wanting?'' that leaves no question about the church's current spiritual condition. In it Mrs. White warned the church, ''In the balances of the sanctuary the Seventh-day Adventist church is to be weighed. She will be judged by the privileges and advantages that she has had. If her spiritual experience does not correspond to the advantages that Christ, at infinite cost, has bestowed on her, if the blessings conferred have not qualified her to do the work entrusted to her, on her will be pronounced the sentence: 'Found wanting.' By the light bestowed, the opportunities given, will she be judged'' (*Testimonies,* Vol. 8, p. 247).

Under a call to ''Repent, and Do the First Works,'' she adds, ''Why is there so dim a perception of the true spiritual condition of the church? Has not blindness fallen upon the watchmen standing on the walls of Zion? Are not many of God's servants unconcerned and well satisfied, as if the pillar of cloud by day and the pillar of fire by night rested upon the sanctuary?'' (*ibid.,* p. 248).

''Who can truthfully say: 'Our gold is tried in the fire; our garments are unspotted by the world'? I saw our Instructor pointing to the garments of so-called righteousness. Stripping them off, He laid bare the defilement beneath. Then He said to me: 'Can you not see how they have pretentiously covered up their defilement and rottenness of character? ''How is the faithful city become an harlot!'' My Father's house is made a house of merchandise, a place whence the divine presence and glory have departed!' '' (*ibid.,* p. 250). And she begins the last paragraph with the words, ''The time has come for a thorough reformation to take place.''

Thus for sixty years God repeated to His people the same message through Ellen G. White—the church was in the Laodicean condition, and was growing more so with the passing years. Heaven kindly let her, however, get a clear view of the grand fulfillment of her hopes before she died; though, like Moses, she would see it in vision only. She gave a graphic picture of what she witnessed. ''In visions of the night, representations passed before me of a great reformatory movement among God's people. Many were praising God. The sick were healed, and other miracles were wrought. A spirit of intercession was seen, even as was manifested before the great Day of

Pentecost'' (*ibid.,* Vol. 9, p. 126).

And so the Great Physician, through His messenger, has for a half century faithfully apprised His church of her maladies —that she is poor, blind, and naked. And that she doesn't know it, which is part of the problem. But hope exists. ''The only hope for the Laodiceans is a clear view of their standing before God, a knowledge of the nature of their disease'' (*ibid.,* Vol. 4, p. 87). First, she must recognize that she is spiritually sick. Instead of saying, ''I am rich, and increased with goods, and have need of nothing,'' she must discern that she is ''poor, and blind, and naked.'' Second, the church must have ''a knowledge of the nature of their disease.'' She must isolate the germ, must know exactly what the spiritual maladies are.

Why do the people of God continue in their deplorable condition? It is a paradox—the inspired messenger describes their condition, they claim to believe her, but they do not know their condition. And how can the paradox continue for fifty years?

Mrs. White offered one reason in 1873. ''I have been shown that the greatest reason why the people of God are now found in this state of spiritual blindness is that they will not receive correction'' (*ibid.,* Vol. 3, p. 255). The kingdom of Israel went into the seventy-year Babylonian captivity for that same reason, as Jeremiah warned them three times in the opening chapters of his prophecy (Jeremiah 2:30; 5:3; 7:28).

Now that the Laodicean has heard that his only hope lies in a clear view of his standing before God and of the nature of his disease, certainly his greatest concern must be to grasp thoroughly just what that message tells him. ''And unto the angel of the church of the Laodiceans write; These things saith the Amen, the faithful and true witness, the beginning of the creation of God; I know thy works, that thou art neither cold nor hot'' (Revelation 3:14, 15).

The Witness stands identified as ''Jesus Christ, who is the

faithful witness'' (Revelation 1:5). And the first claim He
makes is that He knows the true condition of things—whereas
the Laodicean does not. One blunt and positive statement, in
one stroke, sweeps away all the Laodicean's vaunted pride and
self-sufficiency.

"I know thy works." Here is the basis of the Laodicean's
failing. He says he is rich and has no need of anything more.
The True Witness brushes aside all his claims to wealth and
concentrates on his activities. It is by his deeds, not by his
possessions, that the Laodicean reveals his actual state. It has
ever been so. Jeremiah's church leaders felt secure because of
what they possessed. They boasted, "The temple of the Lord,
The temple of the Lord, The temple of the Lord" (Jeremiah
7:4). But the prophet said they must thoroughly amend their
ways and their doings—their works (verse 5). And when the
Jewish leaders flaunted their inherited possession as Abraham's
children, Jesus replied, "If ye were Abraham's children, ye
would do the works of Abraham" (John 8:39).

While the Laodicean church today may comfort herself that
she "is justified by faith without the deeds of the law" (Romans
3:28), she must not forget that both Jesus, the Judge, and Paul,
the great champion of justification by faith, unite in teaching
that man's deeds and actions—his works—determine his ulti-
mate personal destiny (Matthew 25:31-46; 2 Corinthians 5:10).

"I would thou wert cold or hot. So then because thou art
lukewarm, and neither cold nor hot, I will spue thee out of my
mouth" (Revelation 3:15, 16).

Later the True Witness pleads His love for the church. He
says He rebukes the Laodiceans because He loves them. But
here He reveals how He feels because of the church's spiritual
condition: "I will spue thee out of my mouth"—"your
lukewarmness nauseates Me. I would rather you were cold or
hot."

What did the True Witness mean when He stated, "I will

spue thee out of my mouth''? If He is really declaring His intention of discarding His church, would He offer her three detailed remedies for her three maladies? Would He plead His love and call her to repent if she were beyond hope? And would He identify Himself as figuratively standing at a door and knocking if it had grown too late for her to let Him in?

"Because thou sayest, I am rich, and increased with goods, and have need of nothing; and knowest not that thou art wretched, and miserable, and poor, and blind, and naked: I counsel thee to buy of me gold tried in the fire, that thou mayest be rich; and white raiment, that thou mayest be clothed, and that the shame of thy nakedness do not appear; and anoint thine eyes with eyesalve, that thou mayest see" (verses 17, 18).

Thus the Great Physician diagnoses the church's spiritual maladies and prescribes the spiritual remedies. Chapters 10, 11, and 12 will define and discuss the symbols.

We should note several particular characteristics both in the claims of the Laodiceans and the evaluation of the True Witness. Whereas Scripture does describe them as being naked and blind as well as poor, they do not boast of being well clothed and of having good vision. They restrict it to their wealth—"I am rich, and increased with goods, and have need of nothing." The Laodiceans were so preoccupied with their riches that their clothing and eyesight did not enter their concern. Perhaps it would indicate that they considered themselves garbed in righteousness and blessed with ample spiritual discernment, taking such things for granted while concentrating on their wealth. And isn't that just what the church has done, beginning with the disciples down to the present?

The True Witness depicts them as poor, blind, and naked, but first He sees them as being wretched and miserable. "Wretched" is the same adjective that Paul used in Romans 7:24 when he portrayed himself as tied to a dead body. The Romans used to chain a wounded or captive soldier to a corpse and leave him to die: "O wretched man that I am! who shall deliver me from this body of death [margin]."

Wretched, and miserable, and poor, and blind, and naked—five adjectives. And they are used nominally, or as nouns, with only one common article, and addressed with the emphatic "you": "And knowest not that thou [even thou] art the wretched [one], miserable [one], poor [one], blind [one], naked [one]." In contrast with their claim of wealth, the True Witness states that they are poor, and He uses the word meaning one who cringes like a beggar, hence beggarly.

"As many as I love, I rebuke and chasten: be zealous therefore, and repent. Behold, I stand at the door, and knock: if any man hear my voice, and open the door, I will come in to him, and will sup with him, and he with me."

The True Witness has spoken plainly, but He has not left His people without hope. He pointed out the sad conditions, but immediately offered the remedies. "I tell you all this because I love you," He declared. "I stand at your heart's door and knock. If you will invite Me in now, I will invite you later to sit with Me on My throne. Therefore repent. Of what? Repent of your Laodiceanism. And how will you know what that is? 'The straight testimony called forth by the counsel of the True Witness to the Laodiceans' will make it all clear to you."

It will lead the people of God to full victory in their mission. Mrs. White points out the duty of the ministry to proclaim the Laodicean message to the church. Their responsibility she stressed in an 1873 article, "The Laodicean Church," where she wrote, "Ministers who are preaching present truth should not neglect the solemn message to the Laodiceans" (*Testimonies,* Vol. 3, p. 257). "This message must be borne to a lukewarm church by God's servants. It must arouse His people from their security and dangerous deception in regard to their real standing before God" (*ibid.,* p. 259). The frequent use of the word *must* emphasizes the urgency of the minister's

role. Not only within the confines of the Adventist congregation, but also in their public evangelism, the ministers need to
preach it, to center their emphasis around it. "The warning for
the last church also must be proclaimed to all who claim to be
Christians. The Laodicean message, like a sharp, two-edged
sword, must go to all the churches" (*ibid.,* Vol. 6, p. 77).

9. "The Straight Testimony"

"I asked the meaning of the shaking I had seen and was shown that it would be caused by the straight testimony called forth by the counsel of the True Witness to the Laodiceans" (*Early Writings*, p. 270).

Exactly one year after the young church had espoused the revised position on the Laodicean message, on November 20, 1857, Mrs. White received another vision on the subject. It reveals so much so clearly in just three pages that it demands detailed analysis in a separate chapter. The vision appears in both *Early Writings* (page 269) and Volume 1 of the *Testimonies* (page 179).

The chapter begins, "I saw some, with strong faith and agonizing cries, pleading with God. Their countenances were pale and marked with deep anxiety, expressive of their internal struggle. Firmness and great earnestness was expressed in their countenances; large drops of perspiration fell from their foreheads."

The first scene is of a group praying with such intensity as the world has probably never seen except in the Garden of Gethsemane. The description goes on to say that "the praying ones continued their earnest cries." It was not an ephemeral experience.

The second scene, while also describing members of the same church, presents a tragic picture. "Some, I saw, did not participate in this work of agonizing and pleading. They seemed indifferent and careless. They were not resisting the darkness around them, and it shut them in like a thick cloud. The angels of God left these and went to the aid of the earnest, praying ones. . . . And I lost sight of them."

Next the vision presented a third group, also in the same church fellowship. They are the ones who hear the Laodicean message but, like the church in Jeremiah's day, refuse to receive it. "Some will not bear this straight testimony. They will rise up against it."

The vision depicted three separate groups, all church members, separated and formed by their different reactions to the same message. "I asked the meaning of the shaking I had seen and was shown that it would be caused by the straight testimony called forth by the counsel of the True Witness to the Laodiceans." The "straight testimony" would clearly point out the true condition of the church, would force each member to examine his life. Faced with the need to change their lives, many would leave the church. Each church leader, each minister, must ask himself whose responsibility it is to present that message.

"I saw that the testimony of the True Witness has not been half heeded," Mrs. White continued. "The solemn testimony upon which the destiny of the church hangs has been lightly esteemed, if not entirely disregarded. This testimony must work deep repentance; all who truly receive it will obey it and be purified."

Here without question is the most important paragraph in the entire chapter. It states that (1) the destiny of the church hangs on the Laodicean question; (2) it has been lightly esteemed, if not entirely disregarded; (3) it must produce deep repentance; and (4) all who truly accept it will obey it and be purified.

Now Ellen White's attention returns to the first group—the agonizing, praying ones. "Said the angel, 'List ye!' Soon I heard a voice like many musical instruments all sounding in perfect strains, sweet and harmonious. It surpassed any music I had ever heard, seeming to be full of mercy, compassion, and elevating, holy joy." The music came from the group in agonized prayer. They had prayed through to full conversion, as the next paragraph indicates.

"Said the angel, 'Look ye!' . . . I was shown those whom I had before seen weeping and praying in agony of spirit. The company of guardian angels around them had been doubled, and they were clothed with an armor from their head to their feet. They moved in exact order, like a company of soldiers."

Explaining the change, Mrs. White uses three verbs in the past perfect tense: she mentions the conflict "they *had* endured, the agonizing struggle they *had* passed through. . . . They *had* obtained the victory." What was the result of their victory? "I heard those clothed with the armor speak forth the truth with great power. It had effect. Many had been bound; some wives by their husbands, and some children by their parents. The honest who had been prevented from hearing the truth now eagerly laid hold upon it. . . . I asked what had made this great change. An angel answered, 'It is the latter rain, the refreshing from the presence of the Lord, the loud cry of the third angel.' "

Then followed a brief period of persecution when the unbelievers, aroused and enraged by the power possessed by God's people, sought their destruction. But deliverance came. "Soon I heard the voice of God, which shook the heavens and the earth. There was a mighty earthquake. . . . I then heard a triumphant shout of victory, loud, musical, and clear. I looked upon the company, who, a short time before, were in such distress and bondage. Their captivity was turned. A glorious light shone upon them. How beautiful they then looked! . . . This light and glory remained upon them, until Jesus was seen in the clouds of heaven."

And thus ends one of the most thrilling and challenging visions ever revealed to humanity. Every member of God's final church is an actor in the drama. Every one of them will decide, sooner or later—and it is hoped, not too much later —which of the three groups he will join. Will he identify himself with the group that pray through to victory? Or will he, because he is indifferent and careless—the only sins laid to their charge—be among the lost? The vision doesn't say that those in the second category do not pray—rather that they do not pray as the first group. Or will he rebel against the warnings of Laodiceanism to his eternal loss? It is the most decisive and crucial question he will ever face. And no one else can answer it for him.

A careful analysis of the vision reveals the following sequence of events, listed in reverse:

1. The last event is the coming of Jesus.

2. Jesus cannot come until the church finishes the spread of the gospel.

3. But that will not happen until the church experiences what we call the "latter rain," "the loud cry," "the second Pentecost."

4. The "latter rain" will not come until the church has gone through what the early church did in the upper room.

5. That occurs only after a program of agonizing prayer.

6. The church can't pray in such a way until it senses and recognizes its guilt.

7. Awareness of guilt results only through "the straight testimony called forth by the counsel of the True Witness to the Laodiceans."

Another aspect of the shaking process is of vital significance to every Adventist, and should be included here—the sealing of the "one hundred forty-four thousand." Mrs. White equates the sealing described in Revelation (7:2-4; 14:1, 3; 15:2, 3) with that recorded in Ezekiel 9:1-4 (*Testimonies,* Vol. 3, p. 266). In the Revelation account the 144,000 receive the seal of God while the angels hold "the four winds." Then, when they stand on the sea of glass, John hears them singing a song that no one else can learn. Finally, the apostle identifies it as the "Song of Moses and the Lamb."

It is an interesting fact that Scripture presents Moses and Jesus, the Lamb, here as the song's co-heroes. Why? A plausible conjecture could be that it is because they are the two great intercessors of the Bible.

All God's great men were intercessors. Samuel, even after his people had rejected him, assured them, "Moreover as for me, God forbid that I should sin against the Lord in ceasing to pray for you: but I will teach you the good and the right way" (1 Samuel 12:23). Daniel—so blameless that his enemies could find no wrong in him, and his contemporary prophet Ezekiel (Ezekiel 14:14) listed him with Noah and Job as paragons of piety—included himself as guilty when he interceded for his people by confessing their sins. "We have sinned, and have committed iniquity, and have done wickedly, and have rebelled, even by departing from thy precepts and from thy judgments" (Daniel 9:5).

Paul offered to give up his own eternal inheritance if he could thereby save his fellow Jews (Romans 9:3). But the intercession of Moses was still greater. On Mount Sinai God made him a proposition: "Moses, the Hebrews are a rebellious people. Now if you will not interfere ["let me alone"], I will destroy them, and you and your two sons will be the founders of My chosen people ["a great nation"]."

In ancient times every father hoped that his children would develop into a great people. While Moses prepared tables of stone to replace the two he had broken, the two phrases must have kept ringing in his ears—"let me alone," "a great nation." He could remember the insults and complaints against himself and even against God. And he recalled their scornful attitude toward his wife. Yes, he could agree with God—they *were* a rebellious people.

When he went back up into the mountain, he had his speech

all prepared. "Yes," he said, "You were right. They *did* make them a molten calf. 'Yet now, if thou wilt forgive their sin—' " When he realized that God might not forgive their sin, his great heart broke, and he cried out, " 'And if not, blot me, I pray thee, out of thy book.' Forgive them if You can; but if You can't, I want to go down with them." Moses loved his people so deeply that he would rather die *with* them than live without them. Such love and intercession made him a heavenly hero.

The same kind of love and intercession drove the first group depicted in Mrs. White's vision to their knees. It is what makes the 144,000, more than any other of God's people in all ages of His church, His intercessors. Thus they and no others can sing the Song of Moses and the Lamb.

Mrs. White, in discussing the sealing, says, "The true people of God, who have the spirit of the work of the Lord and the salvation of souls at heart, will ever view sin in its real, sinful character. They will always be on the side of faithful and plain dealing with sins which easily beset the people of God. Especially in the closing work for the church, in the sealing time of the one hundred and forty-four thousand who are to stand without fault before the throne of God, will they feel most deeply the wrongs of God's professed people. This is forcibly set forth by the prophet's illustration of the last work under the figure of the men each having a slaughter weapon in his hand" (*Testimonies,* Vol. 3, p. 266).

In the Ezekiel version (Ezekiel 9:1-4) of the sealing, the mark or seal rests upon those "that sigh and that cry for all the abominations that be done in the midst thereof," in the midst of Jerusalem. Mrs. White emphasizes in her next paragraph, "Mark this point with care: Those who receive the pure mark of truth, wrought in them by the power of the Holy Ghost, represented by a mark by the man in linen, are those 'that sigh and that cry for all the abominations that be done' in the church" (*ibid.,* p. 267).

And what are the " 'abominations that be done' in the church"? "Another book was opened, wherein were recorded the *sins* of those who profess the truth. Under the general heading of selfishness came every other sin" (*ibid.*, Vol. 4, p. 384).

The prophecy of Joel makes the call to intercession especially urgent to the ministry (Joel 2:15-17). It summons the church together in a solemn assembly. Bring in the children, even the infants. Interrupt the honeymoon. Then when they are all present, "let the priests, the ministers of the Lord, weep between the porch and the altar, and let them say, Spare thy people, O Lord." Let the ministers take their place between the porch where the people are, and the altar where God is. Then, with the prayer of intercession on their lips—"Spare thy people"—let them reveal their burden, their sense of urgency, by weeping.

Perhaps we can illustrate what must happen to each church member with an imaginary scene. Our hypothetical member sits in his church pew as usual. But today is different. He sees the "sealing" angel approaching him down the aisle. As the angel nears, the man's trepidation increases. Finally the angel stands over him without saying a word.

The church member at last breaks the silence. He reaches into his coat pocket and says, "Here is my tithe receipt. In fact, we pay a double tithe. I raised my Ingathering goal. Last week I gave two Bible studies. We generously support our church, our conference, and its institutions, and our mission program. And we don't . . ."

"That is all very good," the angel interrupts. "But what I want to know before I can place the seal of God upon your forehead is: Are you one of those that sigh and cry about the condition of the church?"

The "straight testimony called forth by the counsel of the True Witness to the Laodiceans" is the responsibility of the church on earth, its ministers and teachers. And the Lord will not return to earth until the leadership of His church responds to "the counsel of the True Witness to the Laodiceans" and gives that "straight testimony" with such power and persistence and clarity that it will lead the church into "strong faith and agonizing cries, pleading with God." Until the church receives, obeys, and lets the Laodicean teaching purify her, she continues to shirk her most immediate duty.

10. Gold Tried in the Fire

"I counsel thee to buy of me gold tried in the fire, that thou mayest be rich." The brief statement points out three factors: The gold must be bought; that is, it will cost something. It must be tested or purified. And it will make the poor Laodicean rich.

Mrs. White stated in 1868, "The gold mentioned by Christ, the True Witness, which all must have, has been shown me to be faith and love combined, and love takes the precedence of faith" (*Testimonies,* Vol. 2, p. 36).

She presented similar definitions through the years:

1873: "Faith and love are golden treasures, elements that are greatly wanting among God's people" (*ibid.,* Vol. 3, p. 255).

1875: "Lack of love and faith are the great sins of which God's people are now guilty" (*ibid.,* p. 475).

1876: "Faith and love are the true riches, the pure gold which the True Witness counsels the lukewarm to buy" (*ibid.,* Vol. 4, p. 88).

1890: "*Faith and love*—how destitute are the churches of these! The heavenly Merchantman counsels you, 'Buy of Me gold tried in the fire, that thou mayest be rich' " (*Testimonies to Ministers,* p. 149).

1898: "Faith and love are the gold tried in the fire. But with many the gold has become dim, and the rich treasure has been lost" (*The Desire of Ages,* p. 280).

1900: "The gold tried in the fire is faith that works by love. Only this can bring us into harmony with God. We may be active, we may do much work; but without love, such love as dwelt in the heart of Christ, we can never be numbered with the family of heaven'' (*Christ's Object Lessons,* p. 158)

The last statement is so challenging and so crucial that we should especially stress it. Regardless of the amount of good deeds one does, no one will enter the family of heaven unless "such love as dwelt in the heart of Christ" also permeates his Laodicean heart.

The place of faith and love in evangelism Mrs. White forcefully emphasized through the beautiful figure, "God bids you with one hand, faith, take hold of His mighty arm, and with the other hand, love, reach perishing souls" (*Testimonies,* Vol. 2, p. 170).

How can frail, selfish man generate such love as dwelt in the heart of Christ? He can't. It will be the miraculous result of the Spirit. "The love of God is shed abroad in our hearts by the Holy Ghost" (Romans 5:5). And when that is accomplished, Jesus will not rest content until that individual, transformed from his native selfishness into His love, sits with Him on His throne. From his honored position of nearness to Christ he will continue, throughout eternity, to marvel at and rejoice in His love. Each one redeemed will realize that he is there because he had become a partaker of divine love—love that will challenge his intellect and thrill his emotions as he joins the unfallen beings and together they "find in the cross of Christ their science and their song" (*The Desire of Ages,* p. 20).

Jesus foresaw such love when, the evening before His death, He gave the disciples a new commandment: "That ye love one another; as I have loved you" (John 13:34). And Mrs. White recorded it when she wrote, "Through the church eventually will be made manifest the final and full display of the love of God" (*Testimonies to Ministers,* p. 50).

The other "element," as Mrs. White terms it, represented by the gold purified in fire is faith. An adequate treatise on faith would fill a large book. We will not attempt that here, but a few aspects of the subject we should discuss in their symbolic setting in the Laodicean teaching.

Many years of preaching and teaching have revealed to the author that most people measure the adequacy of their faith by its size. They do not realize that its direction is the greater factor in determining its power and effectiveness. And the individual will decides the course of one's faith. Many—from youth to the elderly—have cried in despair, ''Oh, if I only had more faith!'' But an honest self-analysis will reveal that the problem is not faith but a perverse will.

Faith comes from God. ''God hath dealt to every man the measure of faith'' (Romans 12:3). (RSV, ''assigned''; Phillips, ''given''; Lamsa, ''distributed''; Weymouth, ''allotted.'') Faith ''is itself a gift, of which some measure is imparted to every human being'' (*Education,* p. 253). What he does with his personal allotment of faith depends upon him. If he wills in favor of faith, it grows. But if he decides against it, it shrinks. ''Everything depends on the right action of the will'' (*The Ministry of Healing,* p. 176). It is the one faculty of which man is sole sovereign. But God will help man even to *will,* if man wants His aid (Philippians 2:13).

When we mention faith, Abraham immediately comes to mind. God promised him and his barren wife Sarah a son when the patriarch was seventy-five years old (Genesis 12:4; 15:4). Ten years passed, but no son arrived. So they contrived a plan to help the Lord keep His promise. Hagar bore a boy, and Abraham accepted him as the son of promise. But the Lord visited Abraham again when he was ninety-nine years old, and He renewed the promise of a son by Sarah. Husband and wife both laughed. ''Lord, I already have a son—'O that Ishmael might live before thee!' [Genesis 17:18].''

Soon after Abraham's arrival in Canaan a famine arose, and he and his household migrated to Egypt. ''Sarah, my wife, you are a beautiful woman and the Egyptians may desire to have you. But we have absolutely nothing to be concerned about, for God has promised that we will have offspring that will possess the land of Canaan. Since we have no children yet, nothing can happen to us.'' That is what Abraham should have said. But his faith was too weak. Instead, he lied about Sarah, saying she was his sister, and Pharaoh had to rebuke Abraham for his deception (Genesis 12:18).

Did Abraham learn his lesson? Years later they went to Gerar, and Abraham and Sarah repeated the same mistake. And again the prophet of God had to receive a reprimand from a pagan king, Abimelech (Genesis 20:9). It certainly was not the size of Abraham's faith that commended him to God. But he finally triumphed in the great test of faith when he ''offered up Isaac,'' the son of promise (Hebrews 11:17).

When Jesus descended from the Mount of Transfiguration with His three disciples, there, among the great multitude, stood a distraught father, seeking healing for his son. Before that crowd Jesus demonstrated what kind of faith is acceptable to heaven. ''If thou canst believe,'' He said, ''all things are possible to him that believeth. And straightway the father of the child cried out, and said with tears, Lord, I believe; help thou mine unbelief'' (Mark 9:23, 24).

The man illustrates weak faith. Jesus could have said, ''If you don't have any more faith than that, I can't help you.'' The father wanted to believe, but he couldn't. Still he used his will to choose to believe. Jesus accepted his small, halting faith. Certainly it grew stronger after he saw his son in the bloom of youth and health, completely restored.

And so, what will transform the Laodicean from his miserable condition into a triumphant overcomer, worthy of a place with Jesus on His throne, is the gold tried in the fire—the riches of faith and love. ''We must buy—'be zealous and repent' of our lukewarm state'' (*Testimonies,* Vol. 1, p. 142).

11. White Raiment

"I counsel thee to buy of me . . . white raiment, that thou mayest be clothed, and that the shame of thy nakedness do not appear."

Many of the Ellen G. White comments, listed chronologically in the preceding chapter, also discuss the white raiment. We will quote just one here because of its comprehensiveness: "The white raiment is purity of character, the righteousness of Christ imparted to the sinner. This is indeed a garment of heavenly texture, that can be bought only of Christ for a life of willing obedience" (*Testimonies,* Vol. 4, p. 88). Mrs. White defines the symbol of the white raiment as "the righteousness of Christ." It is "imparted to the sinner," and constitutes for him "purity of character." "Of heavenly texture," it has "not one thread of human devising" (*Christ's Object Lessons,* p. 311).

Justification by faith in the righteousness of Christ is the most beautiful, the most comforting, the most reassuring, the cardinal doctrine in the Bible. Ellen G. White calls it "the sweetest melodies that come from God through human lips" (*Testimonies,* Vol. 6, p. 426).

Paul, the New Testament exponent of this grand truth, three times quotes the passage that seemed to be the charter of his theology—"The just shall live by faith" (Romans 1:17; Galatians 3:11; Hebrews 10:38). Jeremiah framed the title of Jesus which has become so precious to His people today—"The Lord Our Righteousness" (Jeremiah 23:6). When Paul arrived in Rome the first time, he defended himself before the unbelieving

Jews by saying, "For the hope of Israel I am bound with this chain" (Acts 28:20). What was that hope? Mrs. White identifies it by saying, "Israel were clothed with 'change of raiment'—the righteousness of Christ imputed to them. . . . Here is revealed the hope of Israel" (*Testimonies,* Vol. 5, pp. 469, 470). Righteousness by faith was fully available to the Old Testament church, "But the word preached did not profit them, not being mixed with faith in them that heard it" (Hebrews 4:2).

Paul, having abruptly ended his three years' ministry at Ephesus because of the riot of those supporting the cult of Diana of the Ephesians, journeyed to Corinth. There he learned of the apostasy in the Galatian churches under the influence of Judaizing visitors, possibly from Jerusalem. In sorrow and disappointment he wrote the most impassioned of his epistles. Indignation brought to the surface Paul's doctrine of justification by faith. Some believe that within a relatively short time he wrote the Epistle to the Romans, a church he had never as yet visited. The Book of Romans is the charter of the Christian world on its greatest doctrine, justification by faith in the righteousness of Christ.

In the first two chapters of Romans, he establishes the hopeless sinfulness of all mankind, the Gentiles first, then the Jews. And in the latter half of chapter three and all of chapter four he states and defends his theology, using the experience of Abraham as the vehicle of his line of thought.

"By the deeds of the law there shall no flesh be justified in his sight" (Romans 3:20). Paul condemned the proud and complacent Jewish religionists, who believed that the observance of religious law was the key to salvation. The next verse continues the argument: "But now the righteousness of God without the law is manifested, being witnessed by the law and the prophets." The law points out sin and witnesses to the presence of God's righteousness in the believer's life.

Then Paul proceeds to tell these Jews that even their honored Abraham found his salvation through the same process. In our imagination Abraham stands before the law and discovers himself a sinner. Can he appeal to it for help—"Law, I see I am a sinner. Please help me!" But the law would have to answer, "Yes, you're a sinner, but I can't aid you. All I can do is point out sin and demand righteousness" (see *The Desire of Ages,* p. 762; *Selected Messages,* Book One, p. 367).

But then Jesus appears on the scene. "Abraham," He declares, "this is where I come in. I have righteousness enough for both of us."

"How can that help me?" Abraham inquires.

"All you need to do is to believe that I have taken care of it all," Jesus replies.

Then a third person enters the scene and announces, "You can't do that. That man is a sinner and belongs to me. You Yourself said that 'the wages of sin is death.' Now, You can't do that and be just."

"I believe I can," Jesus answers him, "for you see I am going to die in his place, accept the punishment for his sin. As a result, he will live because of My righteousness." Thus God can at the same time be "just, and the justifier of him which believeth in Jesus" (Romans 3:26).

To establish his thesis that the salvation of man is achieved "without the deeds of the law," Paul continues, "Now to him that worketh [to earn his salvation] is the reward not reckoned of grace [a gift], but of debt. But to him that worketh not, but believeth on him that justifieth the ungodly, his faith is counted for righteousness" (Romans 4:4, 5). Then Paul quotes David in support of the same argument and specifically points out that "God imputeth righteousness without works," and that "the Lord will not impute sin" (Romans 4:6, 8). Christ accepts responsibility for man's sin, and God credits Christ's righteousness to man.

Paul summarizes his argument thus: "Now it was not written for his [Abraham's] sake alone, that it was imputed to him; but for us also, to whom it shall be imputed, if we believe on him that raised up Jesus our Lord from the dead; who was delivered for our offences, and was raised again for our justification'' (Romans 4:23-25).

Ten verses later Paul states, ''We were reconciled to God by the death of his Son, much more, being reconciled, we shall be saved by his life'' (Romans 5:10). His death reconciled us with God; and His life, that is, His righteousness imputed to us, saves us. In that sense the full work of atonement is still going on because Jesus as our High Priest ''ever liveth to make intercession for'' us (Hebrews 7:25).

Let the subject's theological phase conclude with one of the most thrilling statements in the New Testament: ''For he [the Father] hath made him [the Son] to be sin for us.'' Why? ''That we might be made the righteousness of God in him'' (2 Corinthians 5:21).

''Christ was treated as we deserve,'' Mrs. White writes, ''that we might be treated as He deserves. He was condemned for our sins, in which He had no share, that we might be justified by His righteousness, in which we had no share. He suffered the death which was ours, that we might receive the life which was His'' (*The Desire of Ages,* p. 25).

When we respond to Christ and surrender our wills to Him, He *imputes* His righteousness to us, justifying us. That is conversion. Then begins the process of a lifetime experience in which He *imparts* His righteousness to us. That is sanctification. ''The righteousness by which we are justified is imputed; the righteousness by which we are sanctified is imparted. The first is our title to heaven, the second is our fitness for heaven'' (Ellen G. White in *Review and Herald,* June 4, 1895).

After the death of the apostles the Christian church quickly lapsed into the former state of servitude of both Jewish and Gentile Christians. They became ''entangled again with the yoke of bondage," when it was their privilege and God's plan that they should "stand fast therefore in the liberty wherewith Christ hath made us free" (Galatians 5:1). Their tragic apostasy attained its lowest ebb in a few hundred years and plunged the Christian church into a thousand years of spiritual darkness.

Paul's epistles to the Galatians and Romans stimulated the Protestant Reformation. The story of Martin Luther's journey to Rome is well known. He had been teaching Galatians to his university students. In Rome, while climbing "Pilate's stairway" on his knees, the phrase both Habakkuk and Paul used, "The just shall live by faith," suddenly impressed him. He arose from his knees and strode back down the stairs. The Scriptural passage became Luther's watchword, and the Protestant Reformation grew out of the doctrine of righteousness by faith.

The Great Awakening in America began in response to this great doctrine. For sixty years Solomon Stoddard had pastored the church in Northampton, Massachusetts. Its members had lapsed far from the moral and religious standards of their Puritan ancestors. While still religious in outward behaving, they were dead spiritually. Then the old pastor's grandson, Jonathan Edwards, came to serve in his stead. For seven years he preached, but the members remained as lifeless as the pews in which they sat.

In December, 1734, the young pastor delivered a series of sermons on justification by faith. The effect was electric. "The town seemed to be full of the presence of God," Edwards later described the results; "it was never so full of love, nor so full of joy, and yet so full of distress as it was then." "There was scarcely a single person in the town, either old or young, that was left unconcerned about the great things of the eternal world" (quoted by William Warren Sweet, *The Story of Religion in America*, p. 130). The revival fanned out down the Atlantic seaboard, even into staid old Virginia—all because one preacher, with a dead congregation on his hands, presented the doctrine of justification by faith.

Just as the disciples of Jesus did not at first understand the mysteries of the gospel that they were to proclaim to every nation, just so the early Adventist church did not initially comprehend justification by faith, which Mrs. White said "is the third angel's message in verity" (*Review and Herald,* April 1, 1890).

The General Conference of 1888 met in Minneapolis. The presentation of the doctrine of justification by faith in the righteousness of Christ, although receiving great attention, produced varying reactions from church leaders. Two somewhat younger ministers, Alonzo T. Jones and E. J. Waggoner, spearheaded the new emphasis. Their opposition, on the one hand, believed that they had gone too far in stressing their doctrine at the expense of the observance of the law and other traditional Adventist positions. On the other hand, some believed that it was nothing new, that the church had accepted and taught it all along. The close of the meeting left the ministry divided and with great uncertainty. But gradually they accepted it theoretically. But that was not enough. It is not just a theory, but a practical way of life.

After the General Conference session closed, Mrs. White and Jones and Waggoner spent much time together visiting the camp meetings, ministerial meetings, and large churches. Nine months later Mrs. White attested to the meager results of their united efforts when she wrote, "There is not one in one hundred who understands for himself the Bible truth on this subject" (*ibid.,* September 3, 1889).

Soon after, the three separated. Mrs. White went to Australia, Waggoner joined his father in editing the *Signs of the Times,* then labored in England, and Jones returned to denominational headquarters in Battle Creek. Here in the old Battle Creek Tabernacle he continued his preaching, night after night, on the theme that lay heavy on his heart.

He would present a short sermon, then throw the meeting open for response from the audience. A few would respond. One here and another there would stand and, thanking the Lord, would announce that tonight, at long last, he was beginning to understand. But, generally speaking, comprehension dawned slowly.

Night after night a former schoolteacher and devout young woman attended Jones' meetings. Her husband was away in the service of the church. She sat there with a two-year-old baby girl on her lap and expecting another child. Each night she listened, only to leave with an empty heart and a clouded mind. At home she would weep and pray, ''Lord, lead me into the light, or this unborn child of mine will be an infidel.'' Her prayer did not seem to go beyond the ceiling.

Then one night she could declare, ''Elder Jones, I see it now. Jesus took my sins upon Himself as if they were His, and He died because of them. And then He gave me His righteousness as if it were mine. Now I'm going to be saved, not because I'm good, but because *He* is good.'' She walked in the joy and the glow of that wonderful way of life until, at the age of eighty-seven, while her son held her hand and prayed at her request, she drew her last breath. I was that unborn child.

Has the church ever fully received righteousness by faith? An early denominational historian, Arthur W. Spalding, stated, ''The call of God to this church of the last days was, and is, for consecration equaling the consecration of the apostolic church; yes, surpassing it. To this end came the message of justification by faith, a truth never grasped in its fullness by the church of any period'' (*Christ's Last Legion,* p. 38). Then he defines what, in his opinion, that would involve. ''To lose self in the depths of the love of Christ means complete transformation in physical, mental, social, and spiritual habits and activities. The denomination had nominally accepted that doctrine, and individuals in it had gone deep and far, but not deep enough or far enough" (*ibid.*).

Arthur G. Daniells became the president of the General Conference in 1901. In 1924, three years after his retirement, the denominational leadership asked him "to arrange for a compilation of the writings of Mrs. E. G. White on the subject of Justification by Faith" (*Christ Our Righteousness,* p. 5). He authored his book thirty-six years after the 1888 General Conference. Those years included his own administration. Did Daniells believe that the church had received righteousness by faith? The Foreword of his book states: "In our blindness and dullness of heart, we have wandered far out of the way, and for many years have been failing to appropriate this sublime truth. But all the while our great Leader has been calling His people to come into line on this great fundamental of the gospel,—receiving by faith the *imputed* righteousness of Christ for sins that are past, and the *imparted* righteousness of Christ for revealing the divine nature in human flesh" (*ibid.,* p. 6).

"What a mighty revival of true godliness, what a restoration of spiritual life, what a cleansing from sin, what a baptism of the Spirit, and what a manifestation of divine power for the finishing of the work in our own lives and in the world, might have come to the people of God if all our ministers had gone forth from that Conference as did this loyal, obedient servant of the Lord [Mrs. White]! . . . The message has never been received, nor proclaimed, nor given free course as it should have been in order to convey to the church the measureless blessings that were wrapped within it" (*ibid.,* p. 47).

"O that we had all listened as we should to both warning and appeal as they came to us in that seemingly strange, yet impressive, way at the Conference of 1888! What uncertainty would have been removed, what wanderings and defeats and losses would have been prevented! What light and blessing and triumph and progress would have come to us!" (*ibid.,* p. 69).

12. The Heavenly Vision

"I counsel thee to . . . anoint thine eyes with eyesalve, that thou mayest see."

Mrs. White defines the eyesalve in the following five statements. We will quote them in their order: "They will feel the necessity of . . . eyesalve, which is the grace of God and which will give clear discernment of spiritual things and detect sin" (*Testimonies,* Vol. 3, p. 254).

"The eyesalve is that wisdom and grace which enables us to discern between the evil and the good, and to detect sin under any guise" (*ibid.,* Vol. 4, p. 88).

"The eyesalve is that spiritual discernment which will enable you to see the wiles of Satan and shun them, to detect sin and abhor it, to see truth and obey it" (*ibid.,* Vol. 5, p. 233).

"We need to study, to meditate, and to pray. Then we shall have spiritual eyesight to discern the inner courts of the celestial temple. . . . As we apply the golden eyesalve we shall see the glories beyond" (*ibid.,* Vol. 6, p. 368).

"Christ's first words [in the Sermon on the Mount] to the people on the mount were words of blessing. Happy are they, He said, who recognize their spiritual poverty, and feel their need of redemption. The gospel is to be preached to the poor. Not to the spiritually proud, those who claim to be rich and in need of nothing, is it revealed, but to those who are humble and contrite" (*The Desire of Ages,* pp. 299, 300).

The word *discern* dominates four quotations. It would be safe to generalize that the eyesalve gives spiritual discernment, which calls to mind Paul's summarizing statement to the Corinthians: "But the natural man receiveth not the things of the Spirit of God: for they are foolishness unto him: neither can he know them, because they are spiritually discerned" (1 Corinthians 2:14).

The obvious implication in the words of the True Witness and those of Mrs. White's comments is that the Laodicean cannot discern spiritual things. The experience of Christ's disciples who, before their full conversion in the upper room, could not discern or comprehend His teachings about the kingdom illustrates the same point. Mrs. White further indicates in the fifth quotation that God does not and cannot reveal the gospel to "those who claim to be rich and in need of nothing," words lifted right out of the Laodicean message.

Does it mean that the basic beliefs that the Seventh-day Adventist Church has wrestled from Scripture through years of study and prayer are not valid? No, indeed. The Adventist structure of truth came mostly by study and prayer under the guidance of the Holy Spirit, and to a lesser degree by direct revelation through the spirit of prophecy. The foundation thus formed is sound and will stand forever, just as the only partially converted Simon Peter made a pronouncement that Jesus accepted and used as the occasion to introduce the Rock on which He would build His church.

But just as Peter was blind to the spiritual nature of the kingdom, so the Laodicean is blind to much that God wants to reveal to him today. Mrs. White indicates to what a large degree spiritual understanding will flourish when the church applies the eyesalve. "There is yet much precious truth to be revealed to the people in this time of peril and darkness." "The light which God will send to His people will never appear unless there is a diligent searching of the word of truth" (*Counsels on Sabbath School Work,* pp. 25, 27).

"Great truths that have lain unheeded and unseen since the

day of Pentecost, are to shine from God's word in their native purity. To those who truly love God the Holy Spirit will reveal truths that have faded from the mind, and will also reveal truths that are entirely new'' (*Fundamentals of Christian Education*, p. 473).

"We have only the glimmerings of the rays of the light that is yet to come to us" (*Review and Herald*, June 3, 1890).

Such statements, especially the last two, should make the Laodicean humble. But they should also bring a surge of joy and anticipation as he contemplates a rich spiritual future.

Still another aspect to Laodiceanism doubtless contributes largely to the church's blindness. "Light comes to the soul through God's word, through His servants, or by the direct agency of His Spirit; but when one ray of light is disregarded, there is a partial benumbing of the spiritual perceptions, and the second revealing of light is less clearly discerned. So the darkness increases, until it is night in the soul" (*The Desire of Ages*, p. 322).

"Those who have great light and who have not walked in it will have darkness corresponding to the light they have despised" (*Testimonies to Ministers*, p. 163).

"The message to the Laodiceans is applicable to Seventh-day Adventists who have had great light and have not walked in the light" (*Selected Messages*, Book Two, p. 66).

"It pains me to say, my brethren, that your sinful neglect to walk in the light has enshrouded you in darkness. You may now be honest in not recognizing and obeying the light; the doubts you have entertained, your neglect to heed the requirements of God, have blinded your perceptions so that darkness is now to you light, and light is darkness" (*Testimonies*, Vol. 5, p. 71).

Mrs. White said much in her comments on the eyesalve about discerning, especially disguised sin. One does not need conversion to recognize *overt* sin. It is the *inner* sins that the spiritual eyesalve must reveal. Perhaps it harmonizes with the statements thus far quoted to say that the church needs *to rethink the entire subject of sin.*

What is sin? Traditionally we answer that it is "the transgression of the law" (1 John 3:4).

But what is the law? When a lawyer asked Jesus, "Which is the great commandment in the law?" Jesus replied to the effect that there are two, and the second is "like unto" the first: "Thou shalt love the Lord thy God" and "Thou shalt love thy neighbour as thyself" (see Matthew 22:35-39). And He assured the man that the entire law and the prophets hang on one word—*love.* Paul states it simply, "Love is the fulfilling of the law" (Romans 13:10). Now if love is the "fulfilling" of the law, the lack of love would have to be "the transgression of the law" (1 John 3:4). It would seem reasonable to conclude that sin is the absence of love, which would agree with Paul's ode on the supremacy of love in 1 Corinthians 13.

The Laodicean will never fall in love with the righteousness of Christ until he discovers what sin is. He is concerned about his *sins*. But his problem is not that, but *sin*. Not an act or a series of actions, but a condition. The Greek word from which we usually translate "sin" in the English Bible is *hamartia*. It literally means a missing of the mark, a failure to do or be. To be sure, evil acts are sins. But if a man could desist from every evil act and word and thought for, say, ten minutes, he would still be a sinner during that time. He is a sinner because he lacks "such love as dwelt in the heart of Christ." Mrs. White quoted the angel that appeared to her in vision as saying, " 'Lack of love and faith are the great sins of which God's people are now guilty.' Lack of faith leads to carelessness and to love of self and the world. Those who separate themselves from God and fall under temptation indulge in gross vices" (*Testimonies,* Vol. 3, p. 475).

The apostle Paul declared that the law is spiritual, that it is a spiritual document. Jesus earlier taught the same interpretation in the Sermon on the Mount. The law says, "Thou shalt not kill," but if a man hates—the opposite of love—he violates that commandment. A recognition of the law's spiritual nature will change the Laodicean's idea of sin, will lead him to realize that all his moral ethics and Christian service will not save him. It will cause him to grasp in desperation, like a drowning man, for some means of salvation. And that, he will find, is justification by faith in the righteousness of Christ. It has been available and waiting for him all along, but he will not have felt a need for it until then.

"Paul says that as 'touching the righteousness which is in the law'—as far as outward acts were concerned—he was 'blameless;' but when the spiritual character of the law was discerned, he saw himself a sinner. Judged by the letter of the law as men apply it to the outward life, he had abstained from sin; but when he looked into the depths of its holy precepts, and saw himself as God saw him, he bowed in humiliation and confessed his guilt. He says, 'I was alive without the law once: but when the commandment came, sin revived, and I died.' When he saw the spiritual nature of the law, sin appeared in its true hideousness, and his self-esteem was gone" (*Steps to Christ*, pp. 29, 30).

The Jewish nation in Christ's time lost their inheritance as God's chosen people because they did not see the law's true significance. "But Israel had not perceived the spiritual nature of the law, and too often their professed obedience was but an observance of forms and ceremonies, rather than a surrender of the heart to the sovereignty of love" (*Thoughts From the Mount of Blessing*, p. 46).

It is the pride, the self-esteem, of the Laodiceans that especially offends God, that nauseates Him and makes Him want to spew them out of His mouth. Jesus told the proud and self-righteous priests and elders that prostitutes would enter the kingdom of God before they would (Matthew 21:31). Mrs. White drew a similar comparison when she wrote, "Man's judgment is partial, imperfect; but God estimates all things as they really are. The drunkard is despised and is told that his sin will exclude him from heaven; while pride, selfishness, and covetousness too often go unrebuked. But these are sins that are especially offensive to God'' (*Steps to Christ,* p. 30).

In summary, what essentially is the challenge in each of the three remedies that the Book of Revelation urges the Laodicean to apply? The gold tried in the fire is faith and love, love taking the precedence. The white raiment is righteousness, and Mrs. White says that ''righteousness is love'' (*Thoughts From the Mount of Blessing,* p. 18). The eyesalve gives the Laodicean spiritual discernment, which enables him to see the spiritual nature of the law—that the law is love. So the three remedies meet in a common synthesis—''such love as dwelt in the heart of Christ.'' The former Laodicean will then be rich in love, clothed with love, and through the eyes of love he will discern spiritual things.

Then we will see realized in the church the fulfillment of Mrs. White's most exciting prediction, ''Through the church eventually will be made manifest the final and full display of the love of God to the world that is to be lightened with its glory'' (*Testimonies to Ministers,* p. 50).

13. "Thorough Work Was Not Done"

"We have nothing to fear for the future, except as we shall forget the way the Lord has led us, and His teaching in our past history" (*Life Sketches,* p. 196) is one of Mrs. White's often-quoted statements. If it is true, then the converse is also true: We do have something to fear if we forget His guidance and teaching in our past history.

Generally speaking, His *leading* is encouraging and inspiring and a joy to remember. But His *teaching* sometimes contains rebukes and warnings, and one would rather forget them. But to do so is dangerous. Paul, after reviewing the historical failures of ancient Israel, tells the church in Corinth that God had them recorded for their admonition (1 Corinthians 10:6, 11). Similarly, some incidents in our past must serve as warnings and admonitions to the church today. If a historical review can reveal how good men—men who loved the Lord and His truth—sometimes made mistakes and failed to fulfill His purposes, it should help prevent the church today from repeating them.

Thirteen years after the General Conference of 1888 in Minneapolis, another notable General Conference convened at denominational headquarters in Battle Creek. The 1901 General Conference instituted several vital organizational reforms, reforms that Mrs. White had for some time urgently recommended.

First, the session enlarged the General Conference committee from thirteen to twenty-five and later to forty. Second, it set

up a system to equitably distribute the funds to the various
departments and mission fields as the needs indicated. Third, it
approved a plan of organizing groups of several local conferences into a union conference, each under a union president. In
addition, the session consolidated several departments—up to
the time existing as separate organic and legal entities—under
the protection and control of the General Conference (see Spalding, *Christ's Last Legion,* pp. 49, 50). Arthur G. Daniells,
elected president at the meeting, held the position for twenty-
one years of growth, bringing the membership of the church
from 78,000 to 209,000.

But organizational reform was not the only burden that lay
heavy on Mrs. White's mind at the beginning of the conference.
At least as important was the personal Christian experience of
the individual members. Summarizing the situation confronting
the conference, denominational historian Arthur W. Spalding
wrote, "This situation must be corrected; and the correction
involved, first of all, personal conversions, and second, a reor-
ganization" (*ibid.,* p. 40). As he saw the magnitude of the
church's need, he commented, "The call of God to this church
of the last days was, and is, for consecration equaling the
consecration of the apostolic church; yes, surpassing it. To this
end came the message of justification by faith, a truth never
grasped in its fullness by the church of any period. To lose self
in the depths of the love of Christ means complete transformation in physical, mental, social, and spiritual habits and activities. The denomination had nominally accepted that doctrine, and individuals in it had gone deep and far, but not deep
enough or far enough" (*ibid.,* p. 38).

The session convened in the Battle Creek Tabernacle at nine
o'clock Tuesday morning, April 2, with George A. Irwin in the
chair. After the usual formalities, General Conference President Irwin gave his address and announced, "The Conference is
now formally opened. What is your pleasure?" (*General Con-*

ference Bulletin, 1901, p. 23). Then something happened that was not on the prepared program. Mrs. White came forward and spoke to the 237 delegates. Denominational leaders had met informally in the Battle Creek College library the day before at the suggestion of Mrs. White, and there she had given them substantially the same instruction that she now directed to the entire assembly.

The previous year she had returned from nine years in Australia. During that time she had written much, especially on organizational problems and on Christian education. She had completed *The Desire of Ages, Steps to Christ,* and some others. Her personal letters indicated that all was not well in the church in America. O. A. Olsen became president of the General Conference at Minneapolis in 1888 and retained the post for nine years. About midway in his administration he wrote a leaflet, *Special Testimony to our Ministers,* No. 2, in which he expressed deep concern over the condition of the church and especially the ministry. We quote a few statements to show the spiritual pulsebeat during that period and to reveal to what degree the church had or had not received the righteousness by faith experience.

"For three years the Spirit of God has been especially appealing to our ministry and people, to cast aside their cloak of self-righteousness and to seek the righteousness which is of God by faith in Christ Jesus; but O, how slow and hesitating we have been! Instead of feeling a poverty of spirit, and instead of hungering and thirsting for righteousness, we have felt rich and increased with goods, and in need of nothing. The testimony and earnest entreaties of the Spirit of God have not found that response in our hearts that God designed they should. In some instances, we have felt free even to criticise the testimony and warnings sent by God for our good. This is a serious matter. What is the result?—It is a coldness of heart, a barrenness of soul, that is truly alarming. So manifest is this that in many instances our ministrations are a source of discouragement and darkness. The worst of all is, that the situation is not realized. There is a feeling of ease and carnal security.''

Then he quoted the following ''from recent writings from Sister E. G. White'': '' 'If we have the spirit of Christ, we shall work as He worked; we shall catch the very ideas of the Man of Nazareth and present them to the people. If, in the place of formal professors and unconverted ministers, we were indeed followers of Christ, we would present the truth with such meekness and fervor, and would so exemplify it in our lives, that the world would not be continually questioning whether we believe what we profess' '' (compare *Testimonies,* Vol. 5, pp. 159, 160).

Such was the spiritual tone of the church when Mrs. White arose to address the General Conference session, the first such meeting that she had attended for ten years.

She began by calling attention to what should have been done, but was not, during the ten years since the last time she had met with the church's leadership in a General Conference session: ''I feel a special interest in the movements and decisions that shall be made at this Conference regarding the things that should have been done years ago, and especially ten years ago, when we were assembled in Conference, and the Spirit and power of God came into our meeting, testifying that God was ready to work for this people if they would come into working order. The brethren assented to the light God had given, but there were those connected with our institutions, especially with the Review and Herald Office and the Conference, who brought in elements of unbelief, so that the light that was given was not acted upon. It was assented to, but no special change was made to bring about such a condition of things that the power of God could be revealed among his people.'' Note that her burden is that the reproofs and warnings were ''assented to'' but were ''not acted upon.''

The third paragraph begins in the same theme. "Year after year the same acknowledgment was made, but the principles which exalt a people were not woven into the work. God gave them clear light as to what they should do, and what they should not do, but they departed from that light, and it is a marvel to me that we stand in as much prosperity as we do today."

Midway in her thirty-minute address, she stressed further the necessity of acting upon what God had presented to them. "According to the light that has been given me—and just how it is to be accomplished I can not say—greater strength must be brought into the managing force of the Conference. But this will not be done by intrusting responsibilities to men who have had light poured upon them year after year for the last ten or fifteen years, and yet have not heeded the light that God has given them" (*1901 General Conference Bulletin,* p. 25).

The church leaders responded well. The conference closed three weeks later, and toward its close Mrs. White assured the delegation that the angels had been walking up and down the aisles of the Battle Creek Tabernacle during the momentous meeting. The Lord had done His part. Had the church delegates fulfilled theirs? The answer began to come from her pen within seven months, and now appears in Volume 8 of the *Testimonies for the Church.*

In November following the April General Conference session, Mrs. White wrote a letter to the Review and Herald board of directors in which she stated, "If the men who heard the message given at the time of the Conference—the most solemn message that could be given—had not been so unimpressionable, if in sincerity they had asked, 'Lord, what wilt Thou have me to do?' the experience of the past year would have been very different from what it is. But they have not made the track clean behind them. They have not confessed their mistakes, and now they are going over the same ground in many things, following the same wrong course of action, because they have destroyed their spiritual eyesight'' (*Testimonies,* Vol. 8, pp. 93, 94).

She closed her letter by warning, ''If the work begun at the General Conference had been carried forward to perfection, I should not be called upon to write these words. There was opportunity to confess or deny wrong, and in many cases the denial came to avoid the consequences of confession.

''Unless there is a reformation, calamity will overtake the publishing house, and the world will know the reason'' (*ibid.,* p. 96).

Thirteen months later Mrs. White sent another letter to the church leaders in Battle Creek. Dated January 5, 1903, it begins, ''Today I received a letter from Elder Daniells regarding the destruction of the Review office by fire. I feel very sad as I consider the great loss to the cause. I know that this must be a very trying time for the brethren in charge of the work and for the employees of the office. I am afflicted with all who are afflicted. But I was not surprised by the sad news, for in the visions of the night I have seen an angel standing with a sword as of fire stretched over Battle Creek'' (*ibid.,* p. 97).

Then she added a summary of her view of the 1901 General Conference as she now saw it, less than two years later. ''At the General Conference, held in Battle Creek in 1901, the Lord gave His people evidence that He was calling for reformation. Minds were convicted, and hearts were touched; but thorough work was not done. If stubborn hearts had then broken in penitence before God, there would have been seen one of the greatest manifestations of the power of God that has ever been seen. But God was not honored. The testimonies of His Spirit were not heeded. Men did not separate from the practices that were in decided opposition to the principles of truth and righteousness, which should ever be maintained in the Lord's work'' (*ibid.,* pp. 97, 98).

''Thorough work was not done.'' It seems that we can always trace the church's spiritual anemia to that one cause. The

Old Testament prophet Jeremiah declared, "Ye shall seek me, and find me, when ye shall search for me with all your heart" (Jeremiah 29:13). That is the formula—"with all your heart." Here is why the Laodicean message failed when it first came to the church in 1856, and why the righteousness by faith message of 1888 did not usher in preparation for Christ's return. The Lord did not leave the church without a clear picture of what would have happened at the 1901 General Conference if the reformation had been thorough.

After hearing of the Review and Herald fire, Mrs. White wrote to church leaders on January 5, 1903. On the same day she sent a two-page letter to the Battle Creek Church. "One day at noon I was writing of the work that might have been done at the last General Conference if the men in positions of trust had followed the will and way of God. Those who have had great light have not walked in the light. The meeting was closed, and the break was not made. Men did not humble themselves before the Lord as they should have done, and the Holy Spirit was not imparted" (*Testimonies,* Vol. 8, p. 104). "The Holy Spirit was not imparted." Why not? Because thorough work was not done. "I had written thus far when I lost consciousness, and I seemed to be witnessing a scene in Battle Creek," Mrs. White said.

We will not repeat the full vision here, but urge the reader to examine it in full in the chapter, "What Might Have Been," Volume 8 of the *Testimonies* series. The vision centered in the Battle Creek Tabernacle where the General Conference session had convened. A group assembled there, someone offered prayer, and everyone sang a hymn. Then the group engaged in earnest prayer until the presence of the Holy Spirit became evident. Some of those present wept aloud. "One arose from his bowed position and said that in the past he had not been in union with certain ones and had felt no love for them, but that now he saw himself as he was. With great solemnity he repeated the message to the Laodicean church."

The Laodicean message revealed to him his true condition. Then he quoted parts of it, adding, ''I now see that this is my condition. My eyes are opened. My spirit has been hard and unjust. I thought myself righteous, but my heart is broken, and I see my need of the precious counsel of the One who has searched me through and through.''

''The speaker turned to those who had been praying,'' Mrs. White continued, ''and said: 'We have something to do. We must confess our sins, and humble our hearts before God.' He made heartbroken confessions and then stepped up to several of the brethren, one after another, and extended his hand, asking forgiveness. Those to whom he spoke sprang to their feet, making confession and asking forgiveness, and they fell upon one another's necks, weeping. The spirit of confession spread through the entire congregation. . . .

''No one seemed to be too proud to make heartfelt confession, and those who led in this work were the ones who had influence, but had not before had courage to confess their sins.''

Again and again the pattern seems to indicate that the catalyst is confession. Thus the vision ends, and Mrs. White adds, ''Then I aroused from my unconsciousness, and for a while could not think where I was. My pen was still in my hand. The words were spoken to me: '*This might have been.* All this the Lord was waiting to do for His people. All heaven was waiting to be gracious.' I thought of where we might have been had thorough work been done at the last General Conference, and an agony of disappointment came over me as I realized that what I had witnessed was not a reality.''

The last General Conference Mrs. White attended was in 1909 at Takoma Park, Washington, D.C. She was too frail to attend the 1913 General Conference, but sent a message to the assembled delegation. In it she discussed the 1909 session. ''During the General Conference of 1909 a work should have been done in the hearts of those in attendance that was not done. Hours should have been given up to heart searching, that would have led to the breaking up of the fallow ground of the hearts of those who were at the meeting. This would have given them insight to understand the work so essential to be done by them in repentance and confession. But, though opportunities were given for confession of sin, for heartfelt repentance, and for a decided reformation, thorough work was not done" (*Selected Messages,* Book Two, pp. 400, 401).

God's people in the past failed to accomplish God's purposes because "thorough work was not done." Surely His church today needs to examine itself, needs to dedicate itself to repentance, to confession, and to reformation, so that God will not again have to defer His blessing and coming because thorough work has not been done.

14. If I Were the Devil

If I were the devil, I am certain that I would direct my most malevolent ire against those preparing the world for the Lord's return. I would do all in my power to impede and thwart the progress of their church and its program. To do so most effectively, I would voraciously study the writings of Ellen G. White. I would single out those statements that I considered most damaging to me and my kingdom. And as I found them, I would do my best to nullify their influence in the church.

Among the many such passages, I would concentrate on at least three. First, the statement that says that "the destiny of the church hangs" on the preaching of the Laodicean message. Second, the one that states, "Revival and reformation are to do their appointed work. . . . Then a multitude not of their faith, seeing that God is with His people, will unite with them in serving the Redeemer" (Ellen G. White, *Review and Herald,* February 25, 1902). Third, I would note with special alarm the passage that declares, "The enemy of man and God is not willing that this truth [justification by faith] should be clearly presented; for he knows that if the people receive it fully, his power will be broken" (Ellen G. White, in *Review and Herald,* September 3, 1889).

Now if I were the devil, I would divert the attention of God's people from such statements so that they would be "lightly esteemed, if not entirely disregarded" (*Early Writings,* p. 270). And I would suppress the teaching that came to the church in Minneapolis so that it would be true that the "churches are dying for the want of teaching on the subject of righteousness by faith in Christ, and on kindred truths'' (*Gospel Workers*, p. 301). On the matter of revival and reformation, if I had my way, ''there would never be another awakening, great or small, to the end of time'' (*Selected Messages*, Book One, p. 124).

But that would be only the beginning. Some persons always carry a heavy burden on their hearts for spiritual rejuvenation in the church, and they use those three avenues of approach—the Laodicean message, justification by faith in the righteousness of Christ, and a call for revival and reformation. They would be my most serious threat. I would have to silence them or neutralize their effectiveness in the church.

Assembling my satanic hosts, I would announce, ''We will find those persons in the church, disgruntled and critical, those who lust for leadership, and even some sincere in longing to see the full fruition of the purposes of God in His church. Then we will organize them into little groups who will stir up disaffection and call the faithful ones out of the church. And we will have such groups preach so vociferously on the three subjects most dangerous to us that the ministers in the church, especially the younger ones, will be afraid to preach on those subjects lest they be classed with the dissident factions.''

That is exactly what Satan has done—with most effective results. He has created enmity between the groups and the church. It keeps the former from loving the church, and the latter from loving the groups. God's people should always remember that we must love former members, must remind them that God still loves them and wants them back. And we ourselves must remember that many of them united with such a faction because of their concern over the church's spiritual condition.

Let me illustrate my point with a few personal incidents. We were on our way to a General Conference session a couple of decades ago and stopped to visit my wife's sister and her husband. I had just finished my dissertation at the seminary on the Laodicean message in the writings of Ellen G. White, and my wife had assisted in the research. Vitally interested in the subject, she discussed it at length with her sister.

"Our young pastor used to come to see us on Sabbath afternoons, and he would tell us just what you are telling me now," her sister responded. "I asked him one day, 'Pastor, why don't you preach these things in your Sabbath sermons? The entire church needs to hear them.'

" 'If I preached these things in my Sabbath morning sermons, I would lose my job,' he replied."

The minister was mistaken. He would not have lost his job. But the fact that he thought so, sealed his lips.

A few years after the 1888 General Conference, a prosperous Montana sheep rancher named Stanton became quite concerned over his own spiritual state and that of the church. As he continued reading Mrs. White's comments in the *Testimonies,* his burden increased and he wrote a pamphlet entitled "The Loud Cry." As the title suggests, it was a plea to the faithful to come out of the organization—which in his opinion had now become a part of symbolical Babylon—and join a select group.

Mrs. White wrote him a letter from New Zealand early in 1893, the second paragraph of which states, "My brother, I learn that you are taking the position that the Seventh-day Adventist Church is Babylon, and that all that would be saved must come out of her. You are not the only man the devil has deceived in this matter. For the last forty years, one man after another has arisen, claiming that the Lord has sent him with the same message; but let me tell you, as I have told them, that this message you are proclaiming is one of the satanic delusions designed to create confusion among the churches" (*Testimonies to Ministers,* pp. 58, 59).

She also authored a series of articles in the *Review* in which she exposed the error of the man's position. A few excerpts follow. In one she commented, ''In times past many others have done this same thing, and have made it appear that the *Testimonies* sustained positions that were untenable and false'' (*ibid.*, p. 33).

Later she said, ''The message contained in the pamphlet called the *Loud Cry,* is a deception. Such messages will come, and it will be claimed for them that they are sent of God, but the claim will be false; for they are not filled with light, but with darkness. There will be messages of accusation against the people of God, . . . and these messages will be sounding at the very time when God is saying to His people, 'Arise, shine; for thy light is come, and the glory of the Lord is risen upon thee' '' (*ibid.*, pp. 41, 42).

We have no indication that Stanton was not a loyal Seventh-day Adventist. It seems he was truly concerned about the church's spiritual condition. But when he presumed to form a group outside the church body, he was following Satan's course.

During the second world war, gasoline rationing canceled many camp meetings. In one Midwestern conference two ministers held all-day Sabbath meetings in the larger churches. The four sermons centered on the Laodicean message. At the close of one Sabbath the local pastor remarked, ''If these four sermons were preached in every Seventh-day Adventist church, the . . . [he named a well-known dissident group] could not entice a single member away.'' He was probably right.

While I taught Bible in a Seventh-day Adventist college some years ago, a young student, whom we shall call Percy James, decided quite suddenly to leave school during midterm. A few weeks later the president of the college, two or three leading students, the young man's girl friend, and I received identical, full-page letters from Percy. Their letterheads identified them as coming from the headquarters of a prominent dissident group. The letter recited the church's failings and suggested that his group was now providing the remedy. The letters caused quite a stir on campus, and the president asked me to give a chapel talk about them.

"Last week I received a letter from our friend, Percy James," I told the student body. The effect was electric. "I have answered his letter, and I thought you might like to hear it.

" 'Dear Percy,' " I began, " 'I received your letter, and I have read it several times, carefully and prayerfully. You state that the church is in the Laodicean condition. I agree with you. You say there must be a revival and reformation. I agree. You say that righteousness by faith is neglected in the church. You are right. You say that the high standards advocated in the Spirit of Prophecy are not maintained. You are probably right. As you end your letter, you do not say, but you imply, that your organization is God's appointed agency to lead the church, through reform, into the kingdom. Of this I am not convinced. Now Percy, I want to make you a proposition. I want you to write me a letter. In it do not tell me anything of all that is wrong in the church, for on this we already agree. Just give me your reasons for believing that your group is the revival and reformation that will lead the church into the light. If your reasons are convincing, I shall join your group. If they are not convincing, then I shall write you a letter and tell you why I don't think your group is God's agency for leading the church into the light."

More than two decades have passed, but I have never had any kind of reply. The point of the narrative and my purpose in telling it are obvious.

Concerning some of the groups, or their members, we can quote the apostle John: "They went out from us, but they were not of us; for if they had been of us, they would no doubt have continued with us" (1 John 2:19). But they also contain many lonely, honest, searching individuals whom we must love back into the church.

The church Mrs. White speaks of in her reply to Stanton she

identifies six times as the Seventh-day Adventist Church. Let me offer two more quotations, the first depicting the Seventh-day Adventist Church as it is, the second as it will be:

"The church, enfeebled and defective, needing to be reproved, warned, and counseled, is the only object upon earth upon which Christ bestows His supreme regard" (*Testimonies to Ministers,* p. 49).

"God has a church on earth who are lifting up the downtrodden law, and presenting to the world the Lamb of God that taketh away the sins of the world. The church is the depositary of the wealth of the riches of the grace of Christ, and through the church eventually will be made manifest the final and full display of the love of God to the world that is to be lightened with its glory" (*ibid.,* p. 50).

15. "To Him That Overcometh"

"To him that overcometh will I grant to sit with me in my throne, even as I also overcame, and am set down with my Father in his throne." Thus ends the Laodicean message. Divine love can conceive of no higher honor, no more exalted position, than that the Eternal would share the throne of the universe with frail and faulty man, now redeemed by His sacrifice and love.

While it contains warning and reproof, the Laodicean message is one of comfort and hope. "Oh, how precious was this promise, as it was shown to me in vision!" Mrs. White has written. " 'I will come in to him, and will sup with him, and he with Me.' Oh, the love, the wondrous love of God! After all our lukewarmness and sins He says: 'Return unto Me, and I will return unto thee, and will heal all thy backslidings.' This was repeated by the angel a number of times. 'Return unto Me, and I will return unto thee, and will heal all thy backslidings' " (*Testimonies,* Vol. 1, p. 143). The counsel of the True Witness is full of encouragement and hope.

The True Witness, after revealing to the Laodicean church her condition, recommends the three remedies to heal the three maladies, then discloses man's part of the transaction: he must repent—repent with zeal. "Be zealous therefore, and repent." God's people must repent particularly of the Laodiceanism. The True Witness counsels us to *buy* gold. How do we do that? "We must buy,—we must 'be zealous and repent' of our lukewarm state" (Ellen G. White, in *Review and Herald,*

September 4, 1883). Mrs. White says further of Christ's righteousness that it "can be bought only of Christ for a life of willing obedience" (*Testimonies,* Vol. 4, p. 88).

Those who remain careless and indifferent to their Laodicean condition will finally lose their salvation. What does the True Witness mean when He says, "I will spue thee out of my mouth"? Simply that "He cannot present their case to the Father" (Ellen G. White, in *S.D.A. Bible Commentary,* Vol. 7, p. 963). Christ "ever liveth to make intercession for them" (Hebrews 7:25), but He cannot do it for the Laodicean who persists in his present condition. Since, as Jesus said, "no man cometh unto the Father, but by me" (John 14:6), it leaves the persistent Laodicean with no avenue of communication between him and the Father. But on the other hand we must not overlook the persistence of Jesus. "His love is drawing us to Himself. If we do not resist this drawing, we shall be led to the foot of the cross in repentance" (*The Desire of Ages,* p. 176). The Laodicean has choices: repentance and salvation, or resistance and eternal loss. The figure of Jesus knocking at the heart's door implies the Laodicean's need to decide. He will either open the door and let Him in or will refuse to open it.

The Seventh-day Adventist Church began with a small group of believers with great faith and dedication, then retrograded into Laodicean apathy and lethargy in ten short years. But its members did not sense their condition. Then came the warning, "Buy faith and love. . . . Buy the white raiment, which is His glorious righteousness; and the eyesalve, that we may discern spiritual things" (Ellen G. White, in *S.D.A. Bible Commentary,* Vol. 7, p. 964). The challenge briefly shook the church, but then it lapsed into its former Laodiceanism. Here she has remained with greater or less consistency for many years. We have followed the course of every other church —birth, a deeply spiritual youth, and then a drifting away.

But let it be boldly proclaimed that our church will break

free from the pattern. It will end its earthly sojourn in holiness and power and victory: "And in their mouth was found no guile: for they are without fault before the throne of God" (Revelation 14:5). Paul tells of a time when Christ will present "to himself a glorious church, not having spot, or wrinkle, or any such thing; but that it should be holy and without blemish" (Ephesians 5:27). John declares, "We know that, when he shall appear, we shall be like him; for we shall see him as he is" (1 John 3:2).

The church will possess just before Christ returns a holiness such as God's people have never before achieved. "Those who receive the seal of the living God and are protected in the time of trouble must reflect the image of Jesus fully" (*Early Writings,* p. 71). "There will be among the people of the Lord such a revival of primitive godliness as has not been witnessed since apostolic times. . . . At that time many will separate themselves from those churches in which the love of this world has supplanted love for God and His word. Many, both of ministers and people, will gladly accept those great truths which God has caused to be proclaimed at this time to prepare a people for the Lord's second coming" (*The Great Controversy,* p. 464).

As the church received power at Pentecost, so it will be prior to the second coming of Christ. "The great work of the gospel is not to close with less manifestation of the power of God than marked its opening. The prophecies which were fulfilled in the outpouring of the former rain at the opening of the gospel are again to be fulfilled in the latter rain at its close" (*The Great Controversy,* pp. 611, 612).

Miracles and healings will flourish. "In visions of the night, representations passed before me of a great reformatory movement among God's people. Many were praising God. The sick were healed, and other miracles were wrought" (*Testimonies,* Vol. 9, p. 126). "Miracles will be wrought, the sick will be healed, and signs and wonders will follow the believers" (*The Great Controversy,* p. 612).

Prayer will revitalize the church. "I saw some, with strong faith and agonizing cries, pleading with God. Their countenances were pale and marked with deep anxiety, expressive of their internal struggle. Firmness and great earnestness was expressed in their countenances; large drops of perspiration fell from their foreheads" (*Early Writings,* p. 269).

Never before will the church have attained such a capacity to love. The possession of such love will banish human selfishness and implant the Christian virtues. "Through the church [the Seventh-day Adventist Church] eventually will be made manifest the final and full display of the love of God to the world that is to be lightened with its glory" (*Testimonies to Ministers,* p. 50). The demonstration of God's love in the final victorious experience of His church will also exhibit to the watching universe that His dealings with His creatures had been just.

What will bring about such an unprecedented degree of holiness, power, miracles, prayer, and finally the full display of God's love in the hearts of His people? *He* will produce them in human lives. But what is man's part? Repentance, confession, and reformation—not only of the sins of the flesh, but also, and especially with the Laodicean, the sins of the spirit.

This challenge of the Laodicean message is not an issue that lies in the future. It is here, today. It faces every member of the church *now* and cannot be put off. The world cannot wait much longer, nor will the True Witness. The hour of decision crowds in. Note Mrs. White's warning, "And as we near the close of this earth's history, we either rapidly advance in Christian growth, or we rapidly retrograde toward the world" (*Review and Herald,* December 13, 1892).

Which will it be?

It is a decision that only the individual Laodicean can make. And it is the only aspect of the entire process that he needs to concern himself about. If he will surrender his will, the Lord will do all the rest. He guarantees to see the poor, frail Laodicean through to victory. Note the following promises:

"When it is in the heart to obey God, when efforts are put forth to this end, Jesus accepts this disposition and effort as man's best service, and He makes up for the deficiency with His own divine merit" (*Selected Messages,* Book One, p. 382).

"If you will only watch, continually watch unto prayer, if you will do everything as if you were in the immediate presence of God, you will be saved from yielding to temptation, and may hope to be kept pure, spotless, and undefiled till the last" (*Testimonies,* Vol. 5, p. 148).

"As the people of God afflict their souls before Him, pleading for purity of heart, the command is given, 'Take away the filthy garments' from them, and the encouraging words are spoken, 'Behold, I have caused thine iniquity to pass from thee, and I will clothe thee with change of raiment.' The spotless robe of Christ's righteousness is placed upon the tried, tempted, yet faithful children of God. The despised remnant are clothed in glorious apparel, nevermore to be defiled by the corruptions of the world. Their names are retained in the Lamb's book of life, enrolled among the faithful of all ages. They have resisted the wiles of the deceiver; they have not been turned from their loyalty by the dragon's roar. Now they are eternally secure from the tempter's devices" (*ibid.,* p. 475).

Isaiah caught a glimpse of the triumph of the forces of God. "Behold, the darkness shall cover the earth, and gross darkness the people: but the Lord shall arise upon thee, and his glory shall be seen upon thee. And the Gentiles shall come to thy light" (Isaiah 60:2, 3). He wrote about what could have been Israel's story: "O that thou hadst hearkened to my commandments! then had thy peace been as a river, and thy righteousness as the waves of the sea" (Isaiah 48:18). Someday that will happen. As the waves of the sea. When His people respond to His commandments, righteousness, like a tide, will finally conquer evil.

But first, there will be a tide of repentance, a tide of confession, a tide of conversion. Then will follow a tide of prayer —earnest, persevering, agonizing prayer, intercessory prayer—for those within the church and for those without. Then "the people of God are sighing and crying for the abominations done in the land. With tears they warn the wicked of their danger in trampling upon the divine law, and with unutterable sorrow they humble themselves before the Lord on account of their own transgressions" (*ibid.,* p. 474).

The time has come when God will open the floodgates, and the tide of salvation will sweep away all before it. Now all those who have waited, the children who have drifted, the loved ones who have hesitated, the neighbors who haven't understood, the truant members who have strayed, and the hungry individuals on far-off shores—all of them the mighty tide will now sweep in.

> "Far on the reef the breakers
> Recoil in shattered foam;
> And still the sea behind them
> Urges its forces home.
> A song of triumph rises
> O'er all the thunderous din.
> The wave may break in failure,
> But the tide is sure to win.
>
> "The reef is strong and cruel;
> Against its jagged wall
> One wave—a score, a thousand—
> Broken and beaten fall,

Not in defeat, but triumph,
For the sea comes rushing in.
Wave after wave is routed,
But the sea will surely win.

"Oh, mighty sea! Thy lesson
In clanging spray is cast.
In God's great plan of ages,
It matters not, at last,
How far the shore of evil,
How wide the reef of sin.
The wave may be defeated,
But the tide will surely win."

—Anonymous.